Praise For "Think, Write & Retire!"

Let me just say that the resource you're about to read is one of the best starting points for learning the how I've seen. Dr. Mani knows his stuff and he's passing it all on to you here in an easy-to-digest form. It's a wonderful book and I'm quite confident your pocket-book will be greatly enhanced if you follow his advice.

- Mark Joyner, #1 Bestselling Author and Founder **of ConstructZero.ORG**

"Think, Write, and Retire" is a great resource for anyone considering creating a part-time or full-time income from the Internet. Become an infopreneur using the strategies presented here. In addition, learn how to turn your income into good works just like Dr. Mani.

- Terry Dean, Internet marketing pioneer & author

"Every now and then a marketer gets me to stand up and take notice. Dr. Mani caught my attention when I discovered the tremendous work he does to help children with congenital heart defects. But I was doubly impressed to find out that Dr. Mani has used Internet marketing techniques and strategies to bring awareness and raise funds for much-needed research.

A man who lives with passion and purpose, Dr. Mani also understands how to run a successful Internet business. This book demonstrates how absolutely anyone can leverage the power of the Internet to help fuel their passions and live their dreams."

- Joel Comm, New York Times Best-Selling Author of **"Twitter Power"**

D1562718

Everyone wants to know how to make money, how to work online, how to create a 'life' - and while there are hundreds and thousands of experts and technicians... there is no one talking about the importance of PASSION.

More importantly, there is no one LIVING it quite like Dr. Mani. This book is written by a technician with brains, skills AND a heart as big as Texas! A must read in my book!

- Carrie Wilkerson, The Barefoot Executive (TM) & host of **www.BarefootExecutive.tv**

"In this book Dr Mani has compiled all his infopreneur expertise into one easy to consume package. I have never known anyone more generous, he just gives and gives. He gives his valuable expertise, and he gives his profits to charity, so you will be helping yourself on your road to success, and helping a kid live. Who can refuse that?"

- Chris Garrett, Co-author of **'PROBLOGGER - Secrets for Blogging Your Way to a Six-Figure Income'**

"Dr Mani has put together one of the most comprehensive guides to making money from selling information that I have ever seen. 'Think, Write and Retire!' offers the beginner an in-depth, step-by-step guide through all aspects of creating, marketing and then profiting from information products, which in my opinion is one of the best ways to make money available to anyone today. It's a great business model, Dr.Mani is a great teacher and the book is a great buy."
- Yaro Starak, Professional blogger and Blogging coach

"Zero hype, rock-solid information, inspiring truths - and a jaw-dropping opening statement - easily sends this book to the 'head of the class' when it comes to learning how to become an information entrepreneur.

Have you ever wanted to write a book about something, but couldn't get past the question of what to write about? Problem solved – he teaches you how to find your answers in simple, straightforward language with a short, specific exercise that gets your creative thought processes flowing. What if you feel compelled to share what you know with the world, but don't really want to write at all? With this book as your blueprint, you'll be well on your way to helping others learn what you know.

From beginning to end, he shows you step by step, with facts, figures, and examples, how to turn your knowledge into profits, how to create a loyal customer base, find your niche, discover who wants what you have, and how to turn simple ideas of yours into a very lucrative business. This was definitely a "can't put it down" read for me, and I'm certain it will be the same for anyone who wants to get into the Internet information business."

- Tana Stewart

"Think, Write & RETIRE' gave me renewed confidence that nearly anyone can write a respectable info product. One of the most thorough, easy to understand info product development programs I've seen to date. Worth waaaaay more the price!"

- Joe Pass

"Truthful, simple, straightforward, and easy to read and understand."

- G.Sreenivasa Rao

"Of all the things I get regarding internet marketing, I enjoy and learn from Dr.Mani's gifts more than anyone's. Please keep doing what you do for all of us out here. So many of us are frustrated beginners. But then, Dr.Mani seems to realize that."

- Mary Kathryn Donachy

"Interesting and informative. A very easy and pleasing read. I particularly like your decision to include real life examples of your own experiences, such as your early ezine and the plan for your current book.

This certainly helps hold the readers attention and helps to convince the reader that you do know what you are talking about and are writing from experience, not just research. Overall I found the information to be very good, easy to read, informative and in some areas thought provoking. I certainly learned a few things"

- Jeff Collshaw

Dr. Mani's
Think, Write and RETIRE!

Dr.Mani's

Think, Write and RETIRE!

How To Turn Words Into Wealth — Easily!

Dr.Mani Sivasubramanian

Optibiz Mediknow Publishing Pvt. Ltd.
Chennai, India

www.Opti-Biz.com

Contents

A SPECIAL MESSAGE FROM THE AUTHOR

I know you'll love to hear this!

By ordering "Think, Write and RETIRE! you have helped a child live!

It's true. Here's how.

All profits from book sales go to the Dr. Mani Children Heart Foundation, my non-profit organization that raises funds to sponsor heart surgery for under-privileged children with congenital heart defects

Up to now, the Foundation has raised over $130,000 and sponsored 47 operations – all through my infopreneur activities on the Internet. That's the power you'll learn to harness through this book.

And by the simple act of buying a copy, you've helped make a change in the life of a child.

Thank you for that. Now, go tell a friend!

Or better still: order another copy as a gift. Order ten! You'll help more kids.

And then, pick up some great gifts I'm giving all my readers as a 'thank you' for helping spread the word. Go to:

       http://ThinkWriteRetire.com/thankyou.htm

All success,
Dr. Mani

FOREWORD by Mark Joyner

#1 Bestselling Author and Founder of ConstructZero.ORG

That information marketing has changed the world is no longer a big secret.

Times have changed since I wrote what some refer to as "the first ebook" in 1992.

Ebooks are now a common method of reading. Websites are now the standard source of information about a company.

The web is the place you go to dig up dirt on people. And bloggers are often cited as news sources in the traditional TV and print media.

Is it any wonder that people are making money in the process?

The big question for many is "how?"

Let me just say that the resource you're about to read is one of the best starting points for learning the how that I've seen. Dr. Mani knows his stuff and he's passing it all on to you here in an easy-to-digest form.

But will you indulge me for a moment and allow me to wax poetically about the man who wrote it?

See, I'm not so impressed that Dr. Mani has written this book. Again, it's a wonderful book and I'm quite confident your pocket-book will be greatly enhanced if you follow his advice. But to hold this up as the measure of the man is a great disservice to one of the greatest men now walking the earth.

What makes Dr. Mani great is the way he has leveraged his infopreneurship.

He doesn't make a big fuss about it, but he uses the funds he raises with his entrepreneurial endeavors to save the lives of children who really need it. He is a heart surgeon who has dedicated his life to providing heart surgery to children who cannot afford the costs.

This, to me, is the ultimate expression of what the Internet has made possible.

If you think that infopreneurship is all about the spammy "internet marketing" bluster that smacks of a late night infomercial, this might give you pause.

See, online marketing is just a medium. It's what one does with it that matters.

Yes, some use it to send out messages of questionable value, but some are using it to change the world.

I hope it's the latter group who will be remembered, and I hope that you can use the information on these pages not only to change your own life, but to do so by positively changing the life of those around you as well.

Mark Joyner
http://www.ConstructZero.ORG

WARNING - DISCLAIMER

This book is designed to provide information on writing, publishing, marketing and distributing information and infoproducts. It is sold with the understanding that the publisher and author are not engaged in rendering legal, accounting or other professional services by way of this publication. If legal or other expert assistance is required, the services of a competent professional should be sought.

It is not the purpose of this manual to reprint all the information that is otherwise available to infopreneurs, but instead to complement, amplify and suppement other texts. You are urged to read all the available material, learn as much as possible about infopreneuring and tailor the information to your individual needs. For more information, see other resources referenced within the content of this book.

Infopreneuring and information marketing is not a get-rich-quick scheme. Anyone who decides to profit from information marketing must expect to invest a lot of time and effort into it. For many people, however, being an infopreneur is very lucrative and they have built solid, growing and rewarding businesses.

Every effort has been made to make this manual as complete and accurate as possible. However, there may be mistakes, both typographical and in content. Therefore, this text should be used only as a general guide and not as the ultimate source of infopreneuring information. Furthermore, this manual contains data on information marketing that is current only up to the printing date.

The purpose of this manual is to educate and entertain. The author and publisher shall have neither liability nor responsibility to any person or entity with respect to any loss or damage caused, or alleged to have been caused, directly or indirectly, by the information contained in this book.

If you do not wish to be bound by the above, you may return this book to the publisher for a full refund.

Welcome to the Wild, Wacky, Wonderful World of Infopreneuring!

Just over a decade ago, it burst upon the world with the cataclysmic impact of a Force Ten hurricane. It radically rearranged the business environment, creating permanent, irreversible changes in the way marketplaces functioned – globally.

We're talking about the Internet.

And the fuelling force of the Internet is INFORMATION: or rather, data.

What's the difference? Data is the raw, unprocessed, diverse, and disparate collection of bits and pieces of knowledge about everything. It is NOT usable... until it has been processed.

Data needs to be collated, compiled, analyzed, re-ordered, interpreted and packaged into bite-sized pieces that are easily digestible for a consumer, an end-user, a customer.

Enter the INTERNET INFOPRENEUR.

The role is not new. The medium of operation is, however. And by its pervasive, extensive, global reach, the Internet has thrown open exciting new possibilities for an infopreneur – opportunities that can be tapped, exploited and maximized by ANYONE.

Yes, YOU can be an Internet Infopreneur.

I was fortunate to catch this tidal wave almost at the
very beginning. In the early days of the Wacky Wild
Web, in 1995, I tentatively took my first steps into
this exciting medium – and quickly got sucked in by
the tremendous potential in being an infopreneur.

Unlike most other technological or sociological up-
heavals, the Internet information revolution has
kept growing steadily – even at a faster rate than
earlier – for over a decade.

And there's no sign of it slowing down soon!

That's great news – for you. Because even if you are
entering the arena with a plan to become an Internet
Infopreneur ten years later than I did, you still have
a competitive edge that is uniquely your own. You
can easily set yourself apart from the crowd, carve
out your market niche, and dominate it.

The tools, resources and access to experienced mentors and guides are a luxury not previously available. And the medium itself has matured, become
more 'mainstream' than in the beginning, giving
it the 'respectability' many hesitant entrepreneurs
crave before they are willing to step outside a self-
imposed comfort zone.

I encourage you to jump right in. Don't worry. The
water's warm!

Why Should You Be An Infopreneur?

The 'information business' is one uniquely suited to harnessing the global reach and impact that the Internet offers, because it taps right into the major driving energy of the World Wide Web. The Web is an interconnected digital network over which data (and information) can flow without friction over great distances, almost instantly.

Email changed the way we communicate. Online marketplaces changed the way we buy and sell. Web-based communities are affecting the way we interact – even offline, in the real world.

And information shared, exchanged, bartered, sold (and hidden) over the Internet is having a deep and irrevocable impact upon all these areas.

You, as an infopreneur, can be a part of this exciting revolution.

Never before has it been so simple, profitable and inexpensive to take knowledge, experience and wisdom you have or acquire, and turn it into a revenue-generating business – one that can run practically hands-free, on auto-pilot!

What's even more exciting, this business can be managed from wherever you are in the world, all around the clock, day and night, without a staff or employees, entirely by implementing technology solutions to power your enterprise.

The 11 Reasons to Be an Infopreneur

1. You need only your own experience. No extra resources are necessary.

Everything you need to be a successful infopreneur resides right between your ears, inside your brain! In this book, you're going to learn how to extract that precious information, compile it into a product or service, and sell it to the folks who need it desperately. And they'll be willing to pay you for sharing it with them.

These folks could live right across the street from you, or halfway across the globe!

2. Work from home, only in your available spare time.

Telecommuting is all the rage for corporate employees. But you can't beat the lifestyle of an infopreneur. Who else can choose to work in a pinstripe suit in a plush office, or out of their bedroom in pajamas - or even both?

And as an infopreneur, you keep no time, answer to no boss, meet no deadlines, except ones you impose yourself. It's a dream come true for many lazy entrepreneurs.

3. Low start-up cost: affordable for anyone.

Have you ever looked into the start-up costs of setting up a small business in the 'real' brick-and-mortar world?

Depending upon where you live, this will vary; but it's always a sizable chunk of change. There's office space to rent, equipment to buy or lease, employees to hire and pay, legal formalities to complete, licenses to purchase, inventory to stock, manufacturing costs to incur, and a lot more.

When you combine this with the startling statistic that over 95% of small businesses will fail within three years of launch, the low set-up cost of becoming an Internet Infopreneur begins to appear an attractive advantage.

4. Plenty of guidance available from role models and fellow infopreneurs.

Yes, there's no need to reinvent the wheel. Almost every facet of infopreneuring has been explored and experienced by others before you. Luckily, many of them have shown themselves able and willing to share their hard-earned lessons with others... for a price, of course. (Infopreneuring to infopreneurs!)

When I got started selling information products on the Internet, there was barely a handful of courses teaching me what to do. Today, the problem lies on the opposite end of the spectrum, with the bigger problem being how to identify the best, most reliable, valuable courses from the glut out there.

Still, that's a better problem to have than scarcity!

5. Powerful, intuitive, easy-to-use technology available to help you.

Technology has grown by leaps and bounds. At the

same time, smart entrepreneurs tweaked and adapted the tools to further their needs, in the process
making them more valuable and useful to budding
infopreneurs like you.

To take one quick example, look at 'follow up email
autoresponders'. This simple, yet powerful, technology lets you set up a sequence of marketing or customer follow-up messages to be delivered by email
– at pre-determined intervals, AUTOMATICALLY.

You don't need to keep track, and send them out one
by one, manually. Just click a few buttons, and you
have a salesperson conveying your sales message to
qualified prospects on a schedule, 24/7.

It just doesn't get much easier than that. And technology solutions exist for almost every aspect of
infopreneuring today.

6. Can be set to run hands-off, on auto-pilot.

Don't you wish you could be lying on a beach, sipping
piña coladas, while your business chugs along raking
in millions?

Well, maybe you won't be carrying the green stuff
to your bank in sacks just yet. But fully-automated
income streams running on auto-pilot with zero effort on your part are a 'dream come true' for many
infopreneurs - including myself.

Don't get me wrong. I don't mean all you have to do
is wish for it, and checks will magically start appear-
ing in your mailbox. Of course not! You'll need to put
in some effort first: hard work, maybe. But once it's

done, you'll enjoy the fruits of your labor for a long
time – even many years.

7. Scalable: you can take it as high as you want.

Looking to make a few hundred dollars more every
month? You can do it.

Want to replace your day job, and make a full-time
income from your infopreneuring? That's possible
too. It'll be a bit harder, but not very much so.

Do you plan on building your own information empire
online, creating a huge fortune based on your infopreneuring? Even that is well within your reach. Just
know you'll have to do things better, in a more structured, organized, systematic way to achieve this goal.

In the ten years since I started out as an infopreneur,
making many wrong turns, stumbling and groping my
way past a steep learning curve, I have still managed
to create a business that not only meets my needs,
but also helps fund a major project needing huge cash
inflows. My business helps sponsor expensive treatment for little children from underprivileged families,
who are born with serious heart defects.

Your ambition as an infopreneur is only limited by
your imagination!

8. No time limitations. Grow your business as fast or slow as you like.

Tired of punching a clock, turning up at the office
'on time', running on a treadmill that's moving ever
faster, yet going nowhere?

Infopreneuring can be your salvation. You work a schedule determined by yourself, depending upon the targets and aims you define for your enterprise. Big or small, short- term or long, there's a method you'll find optimal and suitable for your work as an infopreneur.

9. No geographic restrictions. All you need is a computer with an Internet connection.

It does not matter where in the world you live. It doesn't matter where, or how often, you travel.

As long as you have access to a computer and a way to get hooked up to the Internet, you can conduct your infopreneur operations unfettered. Indeed, within a short time, you'll learn to set things up so that you won't even need to check on them too often: maybe once a week, once a month, or even once every year!

10. No barriers to entry, such as language, social status, physical handicaps, or anything else.

The World Wide Web is a great leveler. A one-man show can compete on its merits with a Fortune 500 corporation. That's within limits, of course; it's getting harder than before. But it's still very possible – just not as easy as it once was.

You do NOT need expensive tools or equipment. You do NOT need a big marketing and advertising budget. You do NOT need an office, staff, or employees.

You can launch your information business with a

story. Try one based on your own experience, education, or expertise.

11.Potential for passive income for the long term.

To me, the biggest advantage (and one that is often overlooked) is the potential to work once and get paid over and over again. Many people who read about the potential in becoming an infopreneur give up too early, thinking it sounds like too much hard work.

You write a report or book once: and yes, it can be hard work. But guess what? You get paid for that work a year later... four years later... even ten years later, or more! That's FUN.

One of my specialty info-products was created in 2002. Seven years later, I have sold 259 copies at a price of $39.95 each – without lifting a finger, doing nothing except renewing the website domain name every 2 years! That's over ten thousand dollars in PASSIVE income. Sweet!

How Easy Can It Be?

One of the many niche markets I work in is the highly-competitive one called 'Internet Marketing'. Even in such an over-crowded, hyper-competitive area, the principles of good infopreneuring can help you win easily.

As you will learn in this book, to create and sell an information product, you need to

• know what your target market wants, then
• find a solution to their biggest problem, then
• package it into an easily consumed product – and
finally, you have to
• place the offer in front of the right audience to
make sales.

How easy can it be?

Done the right way, it can be VERY easy!

Some years back, I emailed my list of subscribers a
short survey. In it, I asked them what their biggest
problem was. Many said they did not know how
best to take advantage of a new income model that
Google.com (the search engine company), had made
available to website owners. It was called 'Google
Adsense'.

The answer surprised me, as this was an area in
which, at the time, I had limited experience. But
I remembered a few friends mentioning it to me
earlier. A quick email to them confirmed they were
trying out some interesting new ideas, and that they
worked well.

Within a few hours, and with just a few email ex-
changes and a phone call, we had planned a four-
part course to teach my subscribers about Google
Adsense marketing –for a modest fee.

I sent out an announcement to my mailing list of
1,280 readers, and sold out the 47 seats in the class
within 24 hours!

This exercise generated over $1,700 in a day for my business – selling specialized information to an audience that craved it, wanted it, demanded it.

And what's more, I didn't even have to create the information product myself! As an infopreneur, you too can soon be doing deals like this one. It really can be that easy!

Is This the Right Time?

Whenever I talk to people about becoming infopreneurs, I hear two objections, from different sections of the audience.

One group says, "Oh, the time's not yet ripe for this sort of thing."

And the other says, "But isn't it already too late?"

The fact is, there is no 'perfect' time to start being an infopreneur.

Let's face it: there's nothing new about compiling data into information. And there's nothing new about selling the processed product. Why, even the Internet is no longer 'new', though it is constantly evolving.

What is, however, relatively new and unexplored, is the concept of selling information products over the Internet to various niche audiences.

Is the time right to start doing this?

Just look at these numbers.

E-commerce over the Internet in the U.S. for the third quarter of 2006 amounted to $27.5 BILLION, a 4.5% increase over the 2nd quarter and a 20% growth over the previous year (Source: U.S. Census Bureau News, Nov.2006). For this study, e-commerce was defined as the exchange in value of goods and services sold online.

Annual spending per buyer increased from $457 in 2001 to $784 in 2006.

The trend is reflected around the world. Below are the total worldwide e-Commerce Revenues for 2004:

North America	$3.5 trillion
Asia Pacific	$1.6 trillion
Western Europe	$1.5 trillion
Latin America	$81.8 billion
Rest of World	$68.6 billion

(Source: Forrester Research)

So what are they buying? And more specifically, for you as an infopreneur, the important question is whether they are buying INFORMATION.

The answer is a resounding "Yes".

In 2004, more than 14 million Americans made digital content purchases, each for less than $2. TowerGroup forecast that by 2009, the market for micropayments would grow to $11.5 billion in revenue.

One area in which micropayments are growing in the U.S. is for online paid content. According to a

ComScore study conducted for the Online Publishers Association (OPA), the largest proportion of micropayment expense was news (43.8%), followed by greeting cards (14.5%) and games (9.2%). The OPA/ComScore report notes that despite double-digit increase for micropayments, at $12.8 million in revenue, the share is only a 1% of total online paid content revenues. Do the math: you'll see just how vast the potential is for selling content online.

43.6% of all purchases over $50 were made on Business Content. That's good news if you are targeting that market. More and more consumers will buy low-priced content online, with music continuing to lead the way.

In 2005, data from Nielsen NetRatings's Holiday eShopping Index showed a 33% increase in online purchases over the previous year. Books, music, and video combined were the fastest growing category, with a 238% increase.

Are you convinced yet? Or maybe a smaller, more personal sampling will prove the point more forcefully.

In my own infopreneuring business, the revenues and profits from the first half of 2006 were higher than the whole of 2005. A few marketing changes may have had an impact on these figures; but my instinctive analysis is that more people are buying specialized information online, are willing to pay more for useful information, and when satisfied they are getting good-quality stuff, are buying more of it to meet their growing and changing needs.

And that change has doubled my sales in a year!

So, you tell me. Is the time right to start doing this?

What Do YOU Know?
Brainstorming and Niche Research for Infopreneurs

Every single time I've started out a niche market brainstorming session, I ask a group of clients, friends, or subscribers to take out a sheet of paper and make a list of valuable things they know... things that others will pay them to learn.

Nine times out of ten, the answer is almost instant:

"But I don't know anything that valuable!"

Then, for the next few minutes, I explain what we're about to discuss in this section. After a while, their mindset changes and the ideas start flowing.

But don't take my word for it. Try this experiment. Go to someone you know – a friend, spouse, family member, colleague at work, anyone. Ask them the same question: what do they know that's so valuable that people will pay them to learn it?

You'll be surprised to hear a similar answer coming out of everyone's mouth. And that includes folks whom you admire and respect for their knowledge, experience, and wisdom; people you wish you could learn from and emulate!

So before going ahead, I want you to repeat this sentence out loud, three times:

"Everything that has happened in my life is worth money."

Now, say it out loud. Three times. Done? Do you believe it? Well, you soon will.

The 20-Minute Exercise

Now, I want you to take a short time-out for 20 minutes and carry out this simple exercise. Get out a paper and pen or pencil. Jot down on it a list of the things you have learned in your life.

You could go about making this list two ways:

The first way is to begin from early childhood and follow the course of your life sequentially. The other is to recall the most remarkable events in your life, both good and bad, pleasant and unhappy.

Look at the things you've done, your successes and failures, your life's ups and downs. Think about how they have affected the way you are today, and the lessons each has taught you.

Don't worry about how trivial something might appear. If it taught you a lesson, one from which you benefit today, make a note of it.

Remember, this may not be easy work. But it will become the cornerstone of your entire career as an infopreneur, so don't skimp or cut corners. Identifying your strengths and potential competitive advantages is a crucial step to your success as an infopreneur.

Here are some tips to help you get thinking.

• **Start with childhood.** What do you remember about it? Was it good, or bad? And did you learn anything from those events and experiences that would have an effect on the way you raise children today, or advise folks who teach and influence kids?

For instance, let's say you saw a role model constantly smoking cigarettes. That led you to take up smoking, until today you're a chain smoker with bad lungs. What would you tell adults who smoke in front of children to do differently?

Or if you remember embracing your reading habit early in life and realize that it helped change your future... how would you go about encouraging more youngsters to read?

Apply the same rationale even to bad, unpleasant circumstances. Were you bullied or beaten at school? Did you get consistently low grades? Did you hang out with bad company? What did all this teach you? And how will that knowledge be of use to other kids and their parents?

Or even to administrators, counselors, school officials, and care-givers?

• **Think about your education**. When you were in school, college, or even post-graduate studies, what were your most important lessons, insights and critical experiences? What can you remember that others might benefit from? What did you learn (outside the classroom, and inside it) that another student in

your place might find interesting, helpful, and ben-
eficial?

Surely you have wondered, years later, how much
better it would have been if you could have known
about a particular thing, event, or consequence earlier – so that you could take advantage of an oppor-
tunity or avoid a pitfall. Is that information something that is still relevant and potentially useful for
another student like you?

• How about your work experience and jobs?
Recall how you started out, consider where you are
now, and ask yourself how the things you've learned
about could be of value to others.

In today's hectic, rapidly-changing marketplace, job
security and constancy are things of the past. While
your shuffling between jobs might have been viewed
with distaste 20 years ago, surely you gathered some
knowledge and wisdom from these changes. Today,
your experience could serve as an 'expert guide' for
new people entering the workforce.

Did you have a bad boss? How did you handle that
situation? Did it work, or did it NOT work? Either
is fine, and is grist for your information-product
mill. Why? Because by sharing what did NOT work,
you're educating someone who is thinking about
going along the same route, teaching them it won't
work and saving them time, expense, and frustration!

Were you singled out for promotions, transfers, difficult projects, advanced training, or for making
presentations? What did you gain from this experi-

ence? And what were the factors that caused you to be selected for 'special attention'? That could become useful information, too, for others seeking such recognition.

Are you an expert at building teams, or motivating others, or assuring top quality in your group? Do you make friends easily at work, have a system to make your workplace friendly and productive, or a method for organizing your paperwork and dealing efficiently with it?

Every single bit of information and experience you have acquired over the course of your career and life can be the kernel of your budding infopreneur empire. Far too often, we tend to discount and devalue skills and expertise we acquire at great expense, both monetary and personal.

Why do we do it? Because to us, it all appears 'natural': as if everyone else – obviously – also knows it. As if it's nothing 'special'.

But it is special, to others – often, many others.

A friend once told me this: "If you know it and they don't, it's a secret!"

People will pay you for secrets they want to learn!

• Next, look at your interests, hobbies, passions. Are any of them things that many others find interesting too? If yes, what can you share with them that might add fun, enjoyment, or entertainment to their hobby?

Do you know about a secret fishing spot where the trout are really biting? Does your supplier provide you with the finest beads for your costume-jewelry-crafting hobby? Is your brother-in-law one of the best orchid growers and exporters on the continent? That's priceless information for your audience of fellow hobbyists.

• **How about life experiences?** Everyone has them. Some are good, others bad. All teach us lessons. And many people could benefit from your lessons, without having to go through the experience themselves.

Just think. Assume you accidentally ran afoul of a legal requirement and it caused you to shut down your business or pay a hefty fine. It's devastating. But that very information, highlighted to other business owners facing a similar risk, could make you rich – while protecting them from losing their businesses!

Or what if you learned a simple way to beat stress, and that lesson was forced on you by a terrible period following a break-up or divorce. By sharing your system with others, you could do wonders for their health – and your pocketbook, too.

Let's take travel. Do you travel often? What tips and advice can you give others about it? How about listing the best places to visit in India? Or the safest places to eat in Thailand? Or tourist hot spots you simply should not miss in Belgium?

You could even get more general, teaching other new travelers about basic requirements like getting a

passport, buying tickets cheap, getting better rates
in hotels and resorts, and a lot more.

Bottom line: You travel, learn these things by trial-
and-error, and now possess a database of knowledge.
It's the kind of knowledge from which others can
benefit, even profit. Discovering it and identifying
the best way to share it with others is your challenge.

Do you enjoy reading books, listening to music,
watching TV? Movies, shows, musicals, pop groups,
church choirs... magazines, novels, history, classics:
each of these has its own group of fans. They would
love to learn from you what you already know about
their passions – knowledge that will bring them still
greater enjoyment and entertainment.

Maybe you know where to get great out-of-print classics at a discount. Perhaps you own a collection of
vintage records you don't mind lending out for a fee.
Do you have a favorite website you visit regularly for
updates about books to read or music to check out?

Sharing those resources with others who have common interests adds greater fun and enjoyment to
their leisure time. Folks pay money for that kind of
information every day. Why not pay it to you?

Do you have specialized information? It might be
things you know by virtue of where you live, work,
play, or travel; or what you've learned, studied, and
experienced.

Does your job require a refined skill set, like pilot-
ing airplanes or performing surgery or investing in

futures contracts? How about sharing some basics
or the essential requirements of the job with aspiring
students who want to do it on their own?

Can you cook gourmet meals? Or does your special
chicken curry get family and friends in a frenzy?
Recipe collections are hot-selling information products and have jumpstarted many an infopreneur
career.

To put it in a nutshell...

You know a LOT!

And almost everything you know, someone else
wants to know, or needs to know.

Your life experience teaches meaningful lessons.
Your problems and the solutions you adopted to
tackle them are valuable to others. Your contacts,
connections and network are worth a lot.

But not all of them!

That's one of the biggest traps beginner infopreneurs
fall into. They hear about how easy it is to sell information they have. So they skip the difficult research,
and jump right in to create an information product –
based on what THEY think is important.

The lucky ones find out early that this approach
won't work. The unfortunate many spend weeks,
months, even years beating a dead horse – before
giving up in frustration, wondering what people
mean by saying infopreneuring is easy.

Don't make that mistake. Sure, there may be a market for anything you carry in your brain. But as an infopreneur, you want to sort and sift through that vast data bank, and look for the most valuable, most 'in-demand', most profitable information . That's what you'll place in front of the most interested audience.

We'll get into that part of the equation in the next section. But before going there, let's take a look at some basic characteristics of any information that is likely to appeal to a large crowd.

Playing On Emotions to Make the Right Choice

Always remember, as an infopreneur, you are dealing with people. People have emotions. These emotions are powerful drivers, governing almost all decisions they make, including buying decisions.

To be a successful infopreneur, your information must appeal to any one (or better still, more than one) of these very important emotions:

- Fear
- Greed
- Vanity
- Lust
- Pride
- Envy
- Laziness

These are powerful emotions. Yes, they are 'negative', but nevertheless, they are important.

Let's examine some case studies and examples of a few of these factors.

Fear

Do you play the stock market? (Or, to put it more diplomatically, are you an 'investor' in stocks and shares?)

If so, you probably subscribe to magazines, newsletters and membership services that give you stock-picking tips and advice. These are information products, and those selling to you are infopreneurs who often harness their marketing to the emotion of fear.

When you have your money invested in stocks, what are you afraid of? A market crash!

And what if I could teach you how to predict or foresee a coming crash, before it happens? What if I could show you how your portfolio can be guarded against a crash, even if it occurs before you cash out? Isn't that information you would love to own?

I've just played on your fear: fear of loss, fear of being caught unawares, fear of being trapped, financially crippled, going bankrupt.

Vanity

Imagine you look and feel like Marilyn Monroe in her heyday – and are as old as she'd be now. Your friends envy your timeless beauty, your unwrinkled skin, your nimble agility, your bright smile. At the same time, they're sadly making comparisons with their own pot-bellies, arthritic fingers, and asthmatic wheeze when climbing a few stairs.

Now what if you wrote a book showing them how to reverse the aging process, look and feel young again, recapture their youth? What if you taught them how to look like you, even if they are older, weaker, less healthy? Could you paint a rosy picture of a future where they enjoy years of glowing good health?

Will people buy your book? Sure, they'll be lining up all round the block, waiting with cash in hand. Because you appeal to their vanity!

Laziness

You might wonder just how powerful a trigger laziness can be.

A friend of mine wrote a popular book and sold it in electronic format. It taught people who worked at computers, spending hours every day sitting in front of their machines, a simple set of exercises to keep them fit... without getting out of their seats!

It sold like hotcakes, because it appealed to the buyers' laziness. Get fit while you sit. It just doesn't get more attractive than that!

Each of the triggers listed above has similar potency in eliciting a response from prospects. Often, infopreneurs tap into a product idea that appeals to more than one of these emotions, dramatically increasing the profit potential of their creation.

Now that you have listed your experiences, go through them carefully, one by one, and see if an information product based on each will help solve a problem or provide a benefit, while appealing to one of the 'hooks' above. Make a note beside each idea, about which emotions it appeals to.

Later on, when you start looking for a niche to start working in, this will become a major determinant of your final choice. The information product that appeals to the most people will be the one that can pull the most 'triggers'.

Are You an EXPERT?

The single most important thing that will help you acquire more customers, delight them, and keep them coming back to buy more from you is the quality of your information.

And that means being, or becoming, an expert at what you teach.

Far too many infopreneurs are happy settling for being average, or even mediocre. That's sad. Because, even if great marketing and perfect niche targeting allows you to make a few sales and earn some quick money, you are literally shooting your fledgling business in the foot by not delivering top-notch value to your buyers.

So when it's time for them to come back for more information or education, your initial group of customers will ask themselves an important question:

"Did the first purchase give me enough value?"

If the answer to that is "No" - or even, "Maybe" - you
have lost the battle for their mind and loyalty. Your
business just failed!

Does that sound dramatic? It's not.

At best, many infopreneuring businesses only break
even or make only a small profit from their first sale.
The cost of acquiring a new customer is too high.

You need to spend money on product creation, delivery, advertising and other marketing efforts to
acquire your first round of customers. The profit you
have left over barely covers this cost, or gives you a
small return on your investment.

It is only when you delight these customers enough
to get them to come back for more, and spend more
money with your business, and do it often enough,
that you grow bigger and more profitable.

In short, in order to sustain your infopreneuring
business, you need to focus on ALWAYS delivering
top-quality value to your buyers.

When a customer asks himself the question: "Was
my first purchase valuable?", you want the answer to
be an emphatic: "Yes, it delivered MORE than what I
hoped for!"

Which brings me to the point: to delight your customers and over-deliver in value as an infopreneur,
your information must be the best. The only way
that can happen is when the information comes from
an expert – preferably yourself.

So while there are many things in your life and experience that could be packaged into an information product and sold to a hungry audience, not all of them are areas in which you are an expert.

Now, you do not have to be an expert, really. If your network of friends, contacts and colleagues includes experts in a field, and you have access to the information they own and can get their permission to share it with others, then you can be a source of excellent content, without yourself being an expert, indeed even without knowing much about the subject of your infoproduct.

If you decide to go this route, however, keep in mind the potential problems later on down the line when your infopreneur business takes off and grows.

You will soon have a customer base of happy customers who are looking to learn more from you on the topic, or need greater diversity, deeper detail, or other related information. When you depend upon an external authority to confer expert status on your information product, you will continue to be dependent upon that authority for future growth.

This may not be such a bad thing, but being aware of this reality will allow you to plan accordingly. For instance, if you plan a series of information products on a topic, you might want to tie in your 'expert' author to an exclusive (or non-competitive) contract to avoid unnecessary complications from their direct entry into your niche later.

By picking and choosing a subject on which you are the expert, you conveniently sidestep this potential pitfall and become the axle around which the wheel of your infopreneuring empire revolves. Often this means you need to have first acquired the knowledge, expertise, and real-world experience in the area you are teaching others.

To take an example: Donald Trump is ideally qualified to teach real estate investing, and is indeed one of the well known infopreneurs in that niche. But a beginner who is just dabbling in real estate, or has little or no experience handling the complex issues involved in buying and selling real estate, has no business teaching it. At best, by posing as an expert in an area with which you are not sufficiently familiar, you will add no value to your buyers. In addition, there is a very real risk you could harm their future seriously by your misguided attempt.

So even if it appears lucrative in the short term, do not risk your reputation and future business by getting involved in areas where you do not have the necessary expertise. It is far better to team up with a real expert, if you are determined to explore such a niche.

Another way to work around this limitation in expertise is to redefine your niche suitably.

Supposing you want to teach others about investing in the foreign exchange market, but have only two years of your own experience, much of it not very profitable. If you try to write a book about Forex investing for people looking to make a quick, big return in this high-risk environment, you are likely to be quickly shown up – and shamed.

On the other hand, you could leverage your two years of learning and experience to come up with a beginner-level course targeting others like you who are taking their first hesitant steps into Forex trading. Your information product could teach them the essential basics: how to set up a trading account, what issues they should be aware of, how to carry out 'paper trades' to test their aptitude, the best places to carry out online trades, and more.

Always keep in mind that you are the expert to someone about something – because you know things they do not. But at the same time, you are a 'student' who can always learn something more from another 'expert' at a more advanced level than you. Never try and pretend to be that expert; instead, play to your own considerable strengths.

There are some areas where no one is the 'ultimate' expert:

• Relationships
• Time management
• Emotions
• Stress control
• Bereavement
• Parenting
• Mind conditioning.

All of these are 'soft' issues where every person's experience is unique and individual. No matter what your particular circumstances and expertise are, there will be others who can gain strength, confidence, support and knowledge from them.

In these areas, "playing to your strength" can mean

telling your own unique story. Your own life experience, your education, your expertise can supply you with a story that will launch your information business. To start your career as an infopreneur, you won't need an office or employees, a large marketing budget, or expensive equipment. All you need to set yourself up for life in this new career is the right audience: an audience that likes, wants, and needs what you know. Tell this audience your story, and you have your customer base!

In this situation, you replace 'expertise' with another ingredient that's critical to being a great infopreneur: PASSION.

If you are passionate about something, study it with earnest interest, constantly seek to enhance your awareness and knowledge about the topic, keep on top of recent developments, network with other experts in the area, and devote a lot of time and effort to the process, your passion will convey itself clearly to your audience. This will compensate, to a large degree, for your lack of expert knowledge.

It is a truism that if you study anything – yes, ANYTHING – for a few hours daily, then in ten years you will be one of the world's top ten experts on the subject. It is no joke. So, in time, you will really become an expert – and one with passion, to boot!

Who WANTS It?
Core Principles of Finding HOT Niche Markets

Have you heard the saying about "putting the cart before the horse"? Well, that's exactly how most infopreneurs approach their business. It's the primary reason that so many fail at it, or massively under-perform their potential.

The key to successfully selling information products to niche target markets lies in this critical factor:

You Must Find Your Ideal Market First!

Forget about your product. Don't obsess about what you know best. Both are useless without a hungry crowd desperately wanting to buy your information product.

So the big question to ask yourself first is:

Who Wants or Needs What You Know?

Let's assume you've discovered a cure for cancer. Who needs it? People with cancer, of course. Where are you likely to be able to sell water easily? In a desert. Who will buy from your hamburger stand? Hungry folks.

The key to infopreneuring success is locating your perfect prospective audience, people who face a problem that your information product solves, experience a pain that it soothes, or feel a deficiency that it fills.

But that alone is not quite enough.

Your ideal prospect is one who:

- wants your product;
- can afford to buy it;
- has previously bought similar things;
- is willing to spend the money;
- can be identified easily; and
- can be marketed to affordably.

§ § §

What's a 'Niche'?

"Niche Markets" are about a topic, a hobby, or a subject matter in which a certain group of people is interested. There are as many "niche markets" as there are people and interests!

But what matters to you is finding a niche market that is profitable. A profitable niche market is one in which there are enough people who are willing to spend money in their area of interest. They're looking for related information or products or services, which you can provide (or locate) for them.

There isn't any such thing as the "perfect" niche. What's important is how closely targeted it is to your goals.

If you go after a broader, generic niche, you'll very likely have a lot of competition. The narrower and more specific your

niche market, the greater your chances of
being one of a few players in your field –
if not the only one.

For instance, one of my specialized niches
in which I've been operating since 1997
still has very little competition. It is
not a big niche; but because of the lack
of any meaningful competition, I continue
to profit from it without much effort.

On the downside, even if I increase my efforts in this niche five-fold, I may not
get much more benefit from it. If you go
after such niches, you might consider having other niches to work in, so that this
becomes one of multiple streams of income
from your online activities.

§ § §

Who will benefit from what you know?

An infopreneur who plans to launch a successful,
profitable, thriving business begins by asking some
hard questions and finding the answers, before taking the next step.

Often what seems like a great idea is shot down by
preliminary market research. And that's a good
thing. The alternative is to plunge ahead into the
project, blindly, only to discover many weeks or
months later that all your hard work has been in
vain.

So ask yourself questions. Find the answers, or ask
someone who might know. Time and money spent on

the right research will save many times more in the long run.

Who needs to know what you already do?

The simple answer is – anyone who wants to be where you are today, but is not yet there.

If you're a leading lawyer specializing in criminal law, your target market would be law students planning a career in criminal law. If you currently own and operate a thriving franchise business, your market may consist of other franchisees who are struggling to get their enterprise going.

Of course, the caveat is that this group of prospects must be actively seeking the solution you plan to offer. A franchisee who is losing money hand over fist for every day that his set-up is not performing optimally may be a lot more motivated than a student who dreams of a future career, but feels no urgency or immediate pain that needs to be soothed.

Who could possibly be harmed or disadvantaged by NOT knowing what you do?

Going back to the cancer cure analogy, anyone with cancer would be at higher risk if they don't know what you know. The same applies to a business owner who lacks experience in tackling thorny management issues or solving marketing problems that you have dealt with for years, and therefore stakes the survival and profitability of his business on that ignorance.

A very interesting information product I've seen

being marketed is a special report sharing the location of 'speed traps' in specific geographic areas. These 'speed traps' are set by police to catch drivers unawares if they exceed the legal speed limit. The price these drivers are willing to pay to avoid getting caught and being fined gave the product owner a lucrative infoproduct idea!

Another example of this kind of targeting is my wife's short booklet about laptop computer care. By showing laptop owners how to care for their machines and keep them safe, clean, and functioning at top efficiency, this information can potentially save them hundreds of dollars in repairs and servicing.

Who can take your knowledge and experience, put their own spin on it, and obtain a higher advantage from it?

Let's say you're the owner of a lawn-mowing service in Indiana. You have come up with a set of processes (offer, pricing and package) that allows you to get three times more business from your existing clients than your competitors can get.

You could then clearly and explicitly formulate your approach into a system that can be duplicated. You'd include details about how you market your business, what wording goes into your offers, how you present your pricing and packages, and put it all into an information product.

Now, this product could be marketed to other lawn-mowing services in different parts of the country. Business owners in other states would then be able to take your proven system, apply it to their own business, and boost profits. That would let them multiply the investment they made in buying your course.

Or imagine that you run a small family restaurant. You've found that a special offer for free drinks with dinner on 'quiet weekdays' has brought in a surge of new business.

You could detail your approach in a short report, and then sell it or license the information and process to owners of other restaurant chains all over the world. They would be able to leverage your experience and convert it into huge profit surges in their own businesses.

Who else would spend time, money or effort trying to get/discover/find out what you already have and are willing to share?

Just about every niche market has a group of 'do-it-yourself' enthusiasts. Well, maybe there are exceptions – like brain surgery, for instance! Still, you get the point.

Some people like to potter around in their garden. Others like to build their own furniture; or design their websites; or set up their own businesses; or learn to play music.

Let me tell you about how my daughter and I recently went about setting up our own water garden.

The idea came from a book (yes, an infopreneur piqued my interest). So we went out into the garden, picked a suitable place, and dug a hole. We lined it with waterproof material, constructed a stepped 'waterfall', bought a water pump, and tested out the system.

Then we purchased some nice ornamental decorations and some potted plants to surround the water garden. The final touch was getting goldfish for the small pool.

In all, the project took three days and was great fun. Without an information product to spark off that creative thought, and guide us step by step through the process, the lovely water garden that adorns our front yard might never have existed. And without the guidance offered in the book, we might have wasted a lot more time creating it, and the end result might not have been as nice.

Who has a problem, a pain, a troublesome issue that can be solved quickly and easily by the solutions you're able to offer?

My friend suffers severe migraine attacks. Thankfully, they are rare. But when they strike, he's in severe distress. He looks desperately for a solution, needing something to relieve the pain right away.

Imagine: how difficult would it be to sell my friend a book, or even a short report, teaching a method of avoiding migraine attacks, or preventing them from getting worse? All you need to do is get the message about your infoproduct in front of him, and you'll make a sale.

And here's the big point. If you show it to him at the time he is actually having an attack, or soon after, the motivation to buy your solution is highest. But when he is in between attacks, and not suffering agony at that moment, it will be a bit more difficult to sell him your report.

The lesson is to seek an audience or target market that is suffering pain, facing a problem, going through trouble – and at that very moment, offer an information product that teaches the solution.

Who is already desperately seeking such a solution?

So, you think your best audience is made up of people who are facing a problem? It gets even better. Right now, there are people who not only have the problem and need the solution you offer, but they are actively, eagerly, desperately seeking it out themselves!

Those anxious or 'hungry' prospects are potentially the best consumers for your information product.

As an infopreneur, you must look for – and locate – groups of buyers who fit this category. If this group of prospects is easy to reach with your marketing message, you are virtually guaranteed massive success as an infopreneur.

One of my clients sells a report about buying office chairs. That sounds like a weird topic to write a book about. But he stumbled across the idea when he noticed visitors to his website sending him emails asking the same question:

"My back hurts when I sit at my desk for more than five hours. What can I do?"

He researched the topic, and even consulted a chiro-
practor who gave him some tips. After compiling the
information into a report, he shared it with a few of
his readers. Their feedback showed the advice was
helping to relieve their backache.

Using these testimonials from happy users of his
information, he has built it up into a money-spinning
information product that has helped hundreds of
people with backache find comfort and relief. He
has not done much to market the product. His target
audience hears about it from someone who has used
it and found it helpful; and they come to his website
to buy.

Who has benefited from your information in the past? Are there others in a similar category who might do just as well?

A happy buyer is a repeat buyer. When customers
buy an information product from you and it works
'as advertised', there's a good chance they will come
back and buy more – and even tell a few of their
friends about you.

That's why your information must provide real
value. It must

• solve a problem,
• relieve a pain, or
• deliver a benefit.

When it does, your infopreneur business will thrive,
even if you get many of the other pieces wrong.

The nice thing about infopreneuring is that you don't have to stop at delivering value to one market. You can extend the value of your information to other related markets, making suitable changes to your product that will tailor it to their specific needs.

An example may make this clearer. A member in my club is a self-made millionaire. This infopreneur once created a marketing system for restaurant owners. It included a set of things to do, including

- distributing flyers,
- handing out coupons,
- running newspaper ads,
- collecting email addresses and sending out email offers,
- giving special bonuses and extras for first-time clients, and more.

When restaurant owners applied his system to their business, they experienced massive growth. Many were delighted and sent him glowing letters of praise.

Seeing how well it worked in one niche market, he adapted the material in his package and tailored it to other businesses. Soon, the marketing system was being made available in custom versions to dentists, spa and health club owners, and electronic goods retail stores.

The basic information remained unchanged. Minor modifications were made to the material, to target more closely the specific needs of the different fields. Needless to say, this 'line extension' made the guy a small fortune!

Who is paying others to offer the solutions you can provide them, in a way or style that is better, cheaper, easier?

Many business owners research their competition with one viewpoint: to see if they might find it hard to win market share.

However, a crowded niche may not be a bad thing. It is very important that you stop worrying about competition in a high demand niche! Yes, it is possible you might uncover a niche market with very high demand and little competition, but the chances are slim.

Where benefits abound, risks are high too. And where pickings are easy, sooner or later, the crowds will flock. But this is NOT a problem. In fact, you can turn it to your advantage!

The other websites and businesses in this niche are a treasure trove of research data. Look at competing businesses and study how they are doing things. What do they sell, and how do they do it? Who is their target audience, and how do they reach it?

You could look for businesses with which your competitors partner, and then, approach them to be your referral partners, sending prospects to buy from you! Study their process, identify areas of weakness, and see if you can do better.

If there is an obvious flaw or deficiency in their product offering, you can come up with an alternative that's better... or cheaper... or more effective.

If there are areas left uncovered, your product can fill the gap.

If they are addressing a segment of your niche market while ignoring another, you could position your information business to reach that segment.

There are many more ways to take advantage of opportunities in a competitive niche, and position your information product to reach their target audience. Don't think that just because a high-demand niche market already has many players, it is saturated.

This often means there is plenty of profit potential in the niche that you can target. With creativity and sustained effort, you can certainly come up with a way to break in-- and cash out!

The OTHER Factors in Picking Your Niche

While it is important to be able to identify the audience most likely to be interested in your information, that is only the first step. You still have to pre-qualify this group of prospects to see if they will really be potential buyers of your information product. That's when you decide if you should even take the time and trouble to create a product for them.

Why is this important?

I have had clients ask me whether it really is necessary to go through this rather boring, sometimes time-consuming process. And I always answer with a story, and an anecdote from my own early experience as an infopreneur.

First, the story.

There was a young man who wanted to volunteer his spare time for a social cause. He chose to spend three months serving the poor and homeless on the bread-line at his church.

Every morning, come rain or snow, he would be there at the kitchen at 7 a.m. sharp, to serve breakfast. As he ladled out the soup, he'd smile cheerfully at the tired, weary faces of the people who trudged past, asking after their health and making small talk.

Soon he got to know most of the 'regulars' pretty well. Over the next three months, this interaction progressed. He knew their names. He had heard about Jim's recent spat with his wife, Jane's swollen gums, Jack's girl being in hospital and Jill's 'hidden' fortune. He could honestly say he had a 'relationship' with most of these people.

Now here comes my question for you. If this young man wanted to sell his latest information product about investing in stock markets for $97, could he sell it to his 'friends' on the bread-line?

When you've stopped shaking your head, think about how this is different from infopreneuring done the conventional way. See any similarity here?

What matters over and above everything else to you as an infopreneur is correctly identifying, pre-qualifying, and building a relationship with your ideal future customer. No one else. Only potential clients.

Prospective buyers of what you're selling.

Not all of them will end up buying from you. But your task is to try and reach those most likely to do so.

And to do that effectively, you first need to develop a demographic profile of your ideal prospect, and plan your marketing activities to attract or seek only those who fit the bill.

The next story comes from my early experience as an Internet infopreneur.

It was in 1996, and I was rapidly gaining expertise with publishing an email newsletter (or 'ezine'). This is a digital mini-magazine, delivered to subscribers by email, making it simple, cheap, and effective to communicate relevant information and news to a very specific target audience.

My first ezine was about heart disease, one of my areas of specialization and one that I understood very well. Readership grew slowly, and in a year I had over 3000 dedicated readers. They loved my writing. I'd get plenty of email if I missed publishing the occasional issue.

But after almost a year, I had my first reality check. I could not make money out of my list of subscribers for two reasons:

1. I didn't have a product or service my
   readers wanted, and
2. I didn't even know what they wanted!

Finally, in frustration, I was forced to stop publishing the ezine, and moved on to another area. I lost
a dedicated, targeted, responsive list built up slowly
and carefully over time – because I didn't know what
to do with it.

Silly, isn't it? Looking back, that's how it seems today. But there are many others who are in this position now. They are building prospect and subscriber
lists without a clear idea of what they're going to do
with the list, or what their list members are looking for from them. And the only way to avoid getting stuck in this situation is by carefully, patiently,
painstakingly carrying out niche market research.

This means checking whether your prospect, in addition to wanting your information product badly,

• can afford to buy it;
• has previously bought similar things;
• is willing to spend the money;
• can be identified easily; and
• can be marketed to affordably.

Can They Afford It?

Affordability is a serious issue, which is influenced
by many different factors. Most critical to understand, as an information marketer, is that people
will always find a way to buy stuff they WANT as
opposed to things they need.

Many people need to read books on financial discipline and using their credit cards. Most of them do not want such books, but want the latest plasma screen HDTV instead... and willingly max out their credit card to buy one.

Many people need a course on aerobic exercise or a membership to a gym to get their body in shape. Most do not want such a course or membership, but drool over the thought of a triple sundae with extra whipped cream... and conveniently forget about their cholesterol levels temporarily.

Buying decisions are emotional more often than logical, though people need to rationalize a decision made on a whim or fancy. So unless your product is priced clearly out of range of your target market, affordability is an objection you can work around by suitably adapting your offer.

Have They Bought Before?

A good indication that a prospect might buy your information product is previous buying behavior.

People are remarkably habit-driven when it comes to shopping. There are folks who prefer to shop at the mall, others who like mail order catalogs, and some who buy things over the phone after seeing them on TV infomercials. And each prefers their 'channel' to others.

The online buyer of information and physical products over the Internet is also similar. Initial hesitation and security concerns may delay the first venture into online shopping. But a satisfying first experience breaks down resistance, and the convenience, speed, and vast range available to Internet buyers creates loyal repeat customers.

So, as an Internet infopreneur, you should be delighted if your target buying group has a proven record of buying information products in your niche over the Internet.

Are They Willing To Spend?

Markets differ widely in this feature, and each has its own unique price barriers as well.

In a bookstore, a novel or storybook might sell well at a price of $19.95 to $29.95, but rarely more. Go up to $47 and you'll probably kill any sales, unless you are writing a specialty book for an exclusive audience.

In the same way, the general market places an 'average' price limit on information products sold over the Internet. If you buck that range, sales resistance kicks in and you'll have to work harder to justify the price.

People, in general, will be happy to spend money if it either makes them more money, saves them trouble, or relieves pain. It is almost always true that you will get paid to remove a problem, rather than to teach how to avoid it in the first place. Folks will gladly pay for solutions, rarely for preventive measures.

This issue of willingness to spend is, however, not easy to assess. In the final analysis, you're making a judgment call. The only way you can reliably test if your audience is willing to spend money on a product like yours is by actually taking them through an ordering process.

Can You Easily Identify Them?

Some market groups are easy to identify. Passionate fans of video games love to talk about them. They are likely to participate in discussion forums, chat rooms, email lists and other interactive media, where they share their views and opinions about the game.

Sports fans are another easily identified group. So are people excited about politics, hobbies, and pets.

But there are other groups that are not easily recognizable as being parts of a niche – though a little intelligent guesswork will help you identify them. For instance, people who buy baby clothes may be likely prospects for an information product on raising children to be smart and intelligent. Investors in stock markets may be candidates for a course on Forex trading. Frequent travelers might like to learn new languages.

And then, there are a few niche groups that fly completely under the radar, and are either so small, or so well hidden, or scattered and segmented that it is practically impossible to identify them, let alone reach them effectively with your marketing message.

How Will You Reach Them – Affordably?

The best-laid plans could fall down at this point. Nonetheless, this is a crucial question to answer at this stage, unless you don't mind losing money as you're trying to build your business!

If your ideal prospect exists, but you cannot easily find them so as to place your offer in front of them, you don't have a chance of getting your infopreneur business off the ground.

I'll tell you an interesting story, and it has to do with this very book you are reading.

When I first conceived this project, it was meant to target a very specific, geographically-determined audience. There was no book on this subject written for this group of people. I would be able to dominate that niche easily.

Eager to start implementing my plan, I went step by step through the niche research process outlined above. As each of the criteria was fulfilled, I became increasingly excited – until I reached the last step.

To my dismay, my intended target audience was extremely hard to reach! It was so widely scattered and segmented, there was no easy or affordable way to reach it with a marketing message.

There were no common meeting places where this group gathered, online or off. They hadn't many other shared interests. No one had collected names and addresses of likely prospects to whom I could send out an email or direct mail blast. There were no newspapers, magazines, or radio stations delivering niche content tailored to their needs.

If I were to go ahead with my original plan, I would have to waste time and money running untargeted advertising in mass media channels like magazines, newspapers, radio or TV, with a likely low return. It would just be an exercise in futility. So I shelved the initial plan, modified it, and this book came to be written for a more general niche than I first intended. (You really can't tell, now, can you?)

So, even though the information was ideally suited to their needs, and would massively improve the lives of these prospects, the project had to be put off (hopefully, only temporarily) because of logistical problems in marketing it affordably.

Evaluating Niche Profitability

How do you really know if your niche has high enough demand for what you're planning to sell? How can you determine whether it will be profitable for you? Will you be able to guarantee this by following the system you've just learned?

One of the powerful lessons I've learned from marketing legend Jay Abraham is this:

"The only risk you ever have to take in business is an inexpensive test."

There isn't a way to be absolutely, 100% sure... but there are some ways you can get a fair idea about a niche's profitability.

1. Test out your idea on a small scale. Promote your information product to a small, targeted section of your ideal audience. Run a short ad campaign. Conduct a survey. If you get your desired response, you're probably on the track of something hot.

2. Follow the numbers. See who is making a ton of money in your niche. Look at what they're doing. For instance, look at the ads in magazines on the topic. If you see the same kind of ads being repeated, it's probably because they are making money - which means there's demand for the product or service they are advertising.

3. Conduct a formal market survey. Research the demand for what you plan to offer. User surveys, polls, questionnaires, focus groups, and more are research tools in your arsenal, online or off.

Keep in mind the three criteria for a profitable market:

• they must want what you're offering,
• they must be easily reachable, and
• they must have a proven history of paying for what you're offering.

How to Discover Your Niche's Interests

To streamline and refine your strategy as an infopreneur, you'll have to find out what kind of things interest people in your niche, and then go after a segment of that market. Here's one method of doing this.

Let's say that in the course of your niche research,

you run across an interesting phrase related to your
information product. You wonder how many other
people were searching for more information about it
online. You also want to know if there was any potential for profit from these folks and their interest.

1. Log on to the Internet.
2. Go to the Google Adwords Keyword Tool at www.
Google.com to conduct your research.

The direct web link is: https://adwords.google.com/
select/KeywordToolExternal.

In the search box that asks you to "Enter one keyword or phrase per line," type in the keyword you
wish to research. Click the search button, and wait
until the page reloads to see the results of your
query.

After you have made sure that a large enough number of searches is being conducted on that phrase or
keyword, you can progress further. You'll have more
certainty that your niche is potentially viable for
your business purposes as an infopreneur.

Remember, though, that's only the first step. You
should next try to obtain even more data about
exactly what these searchers want, what problems
they are seeking to have solved for them, what benefits they are hunting for.

But how can you do this?

That's when you start examining all the related
search terms that have popped up under your main
search result. Often something startling shows up

when you skim these results, or a common theme emerges. These help give you a better idea of what other interests your niche audience has.

Another simple way is just to ask your audience. You might run a small advertising campaign specifically for the purpose of finding out from your audience what it is that they want.

• What is their biggest problem?
• What keeps them awake at night?
• What solutions are they hunting for?
• What would they like you to do for them?

Asking eliminates all guesswork. You see, we tend to take things for granted. It is almost surprising when someone asks a question – and we remember how, just a few months or years ago, we had the very same problem ourselves!

Yet we don't think of addressing it. In fact, this may be the very problem or solution with which many of your prospects are desperately seeking help.

To conduct a survey on the Internet, you can use one of the many popular survey services. Alternatively, you can set up your own questionnaire, collect responses, and then compile the results to identify the biggest problems and issues you must address while playing in this niche as an infopreneur.

Create an information product or resource addressing those needs, and you'll have a guaranteed winner!

What is the fastest and best way to find out how profitable a niche might be?

Here's a plan of action. I'm not sure if it's the best, but it sure is a fast way to judge a niche's profitability.

1. Decide on your niche – and, if possible, the kind of product or service you're going to offer your prospects.

2. Design a basic sales letter (put it on a webpage if you plan to sell it online), giving some details about the benefits of your proposed product or service.

3. Set up a form or include a tear-off coupon inviting prospects to register for advance notification of the release. You might offer a special discount. If you have a short free report or other grounding material, you could offer that too, as an added incentive to get a better response.

4. Run an online advertising campaign and send visitors to the sales webpage, or mail out ads in the post to potential buyers. Carefully look at your numbers.

If there is a good response to your ads, and the prospects arriving at your web site willingly hand over their contact details and eagerly download your free introductory material, you know this is probably a winner.

If your ads don't get clicked, or if the visitors to your website do not sign up to your free list after reading about your proposed offer, you will find it extremely difficult to get them to pay for it later. In this case, you'll need to modify or totally revamp your plans.

Depending upon how fast you work, you could get this set up on a web site within a few hours, and have your preliminary results in under a week.

If you don't have a project idea, you could even place a form on the website asking prospects to suggest what kind of things they'd consider buying – if you could make them available!

How Can You Share Your Knowledge?
The Many Ways to Showcase Your Wares

Learn the nitty-gritty technical details of packaging and presenting your specialized information in a format best suited to the needs of your target market.

Creating, Syndicating, or Buying Content

The most important asset of your infopreneur business, the reason people want to do business with you, is the nature and quality of your content.

It doesn't matter

- what your infopreneur business is about
- or how pretty your packaging looks
- or that you administer it excellently
- or that you are the top expert in your area
- or that you have hundreds of pages on your website.

The Most Important Thing
Is the CONTENT You Offer!

You'll be judged harshly by your readers. Many of them will be coming into contact with you first, perhaps, by stumbling onto your website. Overwhelming them with exceptionally good content is the only trick you need in your bag to impress them, and then keep them happy, satisfied, and wanting more.

In infopreneur publishing CONTENT IS KING. If you provide content of a consistently superior quality, your business will be a success.

But then you already knew this! What you are looking for in the book that you're now reading is useful
information about becoming an infopreneur.

So, what forms of content should you use as an infopreneur?

A mistake made by many beginners to infopreneuring is that they think about content as being only
text, or words. More specifically, they focus on articles or books.

Sure, words can be content to be sold by an infopreneur. But in a multi-media environment, content
can also be audio or video – even a scent, or an experience, or a memory!

And don't forget that personal, face-to-face, or 'over
the telephone' interaction is content too. Maybe
these are even more valuable forms of content, because your customer now has real-time access to
customized information right out of your brain!

But let's say you want to confine your content to
words. Even then, it doesn't have to be just articles.
You could present words in the form of

- editorials
- news clips or stories
- aggregation of other content
- reviews
- announcements
- periodic updates
- interviews
- interactive features like polls, feedback, discus

sion groups, forums, or online chat .

And these are in addition to books, ebooks, short special reports, white papers, hot-sheets and more.

Does that list give you any ideas? I sure hope it did. Now, let's get into some detail on a few of these forms of content.

Editorials

As an information publisher, you are perceived as an 'expert' in your field. Over time, your readers will begin to trust your opinions and views on issues. You can leverage that status into content for your website or other channels by writing editorials.

Use an editorial to share your viewpoint on a topical, maybe even controversial, issue.

There is an added benefit to this strategy. Readers will respond to your message, either to endorse it or oppose it. Their feedback can be incorporated into a follow-up article or report, adding fresh content to your storehouse!

You could also use the editorial space to establish personal contact with your readers. Write about your clients, subscribers, friends, or other contacts in your area of interest. In addition, invite readers to share an experience with you.

Notice how I'm sprinkling in stories of other infopreneur successes of which I'm aware, or which I helped create? This is an example of the technique mentioned above.

Always think about creating content that can keep
growing by means of reader-generated input.

News Clips and Stories

Staying abreast of the latest developments and news
in specialized areas is becoming increasingly difficult
and time-consuming. Your content can take the form
of offering a solution by providing timely news on
topics that might be of interest to your readers.

With the array of web-based content aggregation
tools currently available, doing this is no longer
time- and effort-intensive as it once was. A bonus is
that it generates automatically-growing content for
your website.

You can set yourself apart from others who are using
the same material by the way you choose to present the news. Make sure to stamp it with your own
personality. Be interesting, personal, chatty, fun,
unique, or all of these – with your style of writing, or
by adding your point of view.

One of the best-selling business books was a review
of other business books. Instead of original concepts
and newest industry buzzwords, this book was made
up of condensed, one-page summaries of the most
powerful lessons contained in other business books.

By saving a reader time spent on poring over 100
other business books, and by providing them with
the gist of the material in brief, easily-digestible
form, this book captured a niche and dominated it.
It was perfect for busy business people looking to

widen their knowledge base.

A friend of mine is now extending this model to the Internet.

With the explosion of e-publishing, there are literally hundreds of email news-letters in many popular niches. For a keen prospect who wants to stay informed about the newest, hottest, most profitable developments, the cost in time and effort is massive.

One guy is offering something like a news clipping service for this market. But he adds a spin. Being a fellow enthusiast in the same niche, and an expert in the subject matter, he is able to weed through the useless information, process what's left, and review it for suitability and value to his audience.

He then compiles the best stories, news items and breakthroughs into a separate publication, with his comments and opinions on the best ones, and distributes it to the other players in the niche. These folks eagerly snap up subscriptions at a fair annual subscription fee.

This is classic infopreneur behavior:

- Identify a market.
- Take your expertise to it.
- Create a unique information product.
- Sell it to the market that already wants it.

Aggregating Useful Content

Many readers will appreciate a listing of helpful resources on a subject.

'Top 5 Website Picks' is a great content idea for your own site. 'Best Books Reviewed' or 'Best Seminars to Attend' or 'Top Experts to Learn From' are others you can use.

As an expert on your topic, you can evaluate resources (ezines, directories, books, offline publications, conferences, mentoring programs) and post short reviews of the ones you think most useful. This information would become a valuable guide to beginners who will benefit from what you share.

If you don't fancy the idea of doing it yourself, online content aggregation tools based on RSS feeds can help automate the technical side of things. It takes some time to locate good sources that offer valuable information on a consistent basis. However, once you've found them, the technology exists to automatically monitor updates to content on those sites, and keep you informed from time to time.

Reviews

Here's your chance to help your readers by guiding them to the very best books, websites, music, or other products and services. You, the expert, tell your audience what is good and what isn't.

A guiding principle in writing reviews is that the reader's need comes first. In a review, you share something that will be of interest and benefit to readers. If you read a great book, or happen to find a wonderful website, then tell your audience about it in a review.

The Inn at Lambertville Station

11 Bridge Street
Lambertville, New Jersey 08530
609-397-4400   1-800-524-1091

ADDRESS

How to write a review? Here are some tips:

• Be brief. Provide contact / ordering information
for those who want to know more.
• Be relevant. Limit your reviews to the topic and
subject of your website.
• Be selective. Set high standards for the products
you review. A positive review by you should be
come an honor people will hunger for!
• Be analytical. Tell your reader specifically what
is good or bad about the thing you review.
• Don't go overboard. Restrain your impulse to offer
extremes of praise and criticism.
• Be balanced. Point out the good and bad aspects
with equal emphasis.
• Offer recommendations. At the end, say what you
think about it. Is it good, or bad? Should your
reader buy the product, visit the website, order the
service? Tell them.

Just remember to stay within the guidelines: relevant and useful to your reader.

To take it a step further, you could solicit feedback on
the reviews you create.

Ask readers to let you know if they liked what you
created. Amazon.com lets you rate the usefulness of
reviews. Some sites let you debate them. All of this
automatically adds fresh content to your website –
without you having to write a word!

Announcements

Some innovative infopreneurs use information on
recent happenings in a company, industry, or a spe-

cific part of the world, and build information empires
around it.

Has your business done something new and innova-
tive?
Have you developed an improved version of your
product or service?
Are you privy to insider information in your indus-
try?
Do you follow the rumors and gossip in your field?
Do you track swings and developments closely?

If you do, announce them – and sell access to announcements to anyone who will pay you for it!

Interviews

Publishing an interview with an expert provides
exciting, valuable content. It is easy to conduct such
an interview via e-mail or on the phone.

Step 1:   Identify your expert.

Step 2:   Learn more about your expert. Check on
special interests, experience, achievements, status in
field, etc. This allows you to tailor your interview to
suit the individual.

Step 3:   Decide upon a topic for the interview. Prepare a set of questions you'd like to ask.

Step 4:   Contact your expert with an interview
request. Most experts will be happy to participate in
your interview. For those who seem hesitant, mention the publicity they will get from your marketing,
or offer a freebie or gift to get them to agree. You

might even offer to pay them for their time.

Step 5:   Send your questions to the expert and review the reply. Make editorial changes suitable for
your readership. Rearrange the questions so that
the thoughts flow smoothly. By intelligently juggling
the content around, and sprinkling in additional que-
ries and comments, you can make it appear as if the
interview was carried out in person, even if you did
it by email! Ask more questions, or get clarifications
when necessary.

Step 6:   Get approval from your expert for the final
version of the interview.

Step 7:   PUBLISH !

Letting Users Create Your Content

What I'm about to tell you in this section is explo-
sively powerful stuff that has the potential to save
you time and effort while creating your content. Best
of all, it will guarantee your Internet infopreneur
business will grow and expand, literally on auto-
pilot.

The Key Is To Create Interactive Features

What sets apart the Internet and e-mail from traditional media (television, radio, newspaper, and
magazines) is the potential for 'two-way' communication, or reader interactivity. And this is easy for an
Internet infopreneur to incorporate on a website.

Why should you interact with readers through the

Internet? The most important reason is because it will improve your website's quality.

• You can establish closer, more personal relationships with visitors.
• You can find out about their preferences, likes, and dislikes.
• You can listen to their complaints and suggestions.
• You can request their feedback on your performance.
• You can collect valuable demographic data on your audience.

All of this allows you to make improvements and additions. You can enhance the value and utility of your website and your content, as well as make it more specific, useful, and desirable to your reader. Plus, you can get fresh content to use on your website!

How to do it? Here are a few ideas:

Conduct Surveys and Polls

Survey your readers. Ask a question. Request a vote on an issue or topic. You can seek feedback about anything:

• an article on your website. "Did you find this week's feature helpful?"
• current events. "Do you agree with the latest CAN-SPAM legislation?"
• a controversial issue. "Should prayer in schools be made compulsory?"
• user preferences. "Would you like to receive this

ezine every week or daily?"
• demographic data. "Do you have young children?"

Don't overdo it, however.

• Be imaginative and creative.
• Be brief. Ask no more than seven or eight questions.
 • Offer choices. Frame the questions to have a YES/
NO option.
• Provide an incentive to reply – a discount, a freebie, a trial membership.

Compile the results and announce them to the list.
Your readers will enjoy hearing what their peers
think and feel about these issues. And you just created another form in which your content can be
packaged!

Seek User Feedback

Reader feedback is extremely valuable. However, you
need to listen to it with a mind open to change, and
act on the suggestions your readers offer. The right
kind of feedback can become valuable content to add
to your website.

How can you get feedback from your reader?

• Make it obvious that you welcome feedback. Place
easy-to-find links on your website, or on a forum or
blog, so readers can easily click to post their suggestions or comments, or to send you email.

• Actively ask readers to write back with their comments, opinions and suggestions for improvement.

How do you turn feedback into content?

There are many different ways to do it. Use your
imagination. Here are some thoughts:

• Blog comments. If you have enabled visitors to
your blog to leave comments, each message or feedback is appended to your initial blog post, and automatically displayed, becoming fresh content for your
blog.

• Forum posts. Your site visitors can be invited to
share their thoughts on a discussion board where
others can read it. A lively debate might ensue.

• Use an HTML 'form to web page' script (like a
Guestbook) so user- generated feedback is posted
instantly to your web page.

• Compile feedback into an article or add-on report,
and link it from the original article that generated
the feedback

Discussion Lists

Building a discussion group around your topic is another way to promote interactivity, while generating
usable content in the process. The group may be web-
based (forums and bulletin boards) or email based.

While feedback is one-to-one communication, a discussion group permits many-to-many interaction,
since every e-mail sent to the group is distributed to
each member.

The material generated in discussions and debate

can be used as content for your website.

Chat Rooms

Real-time online chat is a fantastic interactive tool —
but it has some unavoidable limitations.

Chat rooms allow interaction with your readers.
However, they can become serious time-wasters unless you are disciplined and well organized. Other
inconveniences include time zone differences across
countries, dependence on technology, and problems
with scheduling times when many participants are
available.

Chat events permit the creation of innovative content like

• interviews with participants, especially experts
and celebrities;
• discussions on featured topics and issues; and
• workshops and seminars for website readers.

Transcripts of chat sessions (edited for continuity
and flow of the conversation) make for exciting content

Audio and Video Content

Almost every kind of content we just talked about
can be made available in audio and video format.
The converse is also true: if you create audio or video
content, it can be transcribed into words.

Why would you prefer one form over another?

That's simple: because your buyers have different preferences.

People learn, consume information, and enjoy entertainment in various forms. Some are audiocentric, and like auditory content – music, audio books, interviews, seminars, or teleconferences. Others learn visually, and prefer movies, how-to video tutorials, and instruction manuals full of pictures and graphics. And a portion of your customer base will learn best by reading; they will devour your content when it is presented as written words.

Depending on your audience, your own product creation preferences, and how deeply and intensely you want to touch your market, you as an infopreneur must consider creating your content in all three forms – and any other your audience prefers, wants, and is used to consuming.

With the advent of powerful tools to create multimedia content, and computers capable of running professional-quality movie-making and sound-recording software, the cost and complexity of recording audio and video information products has become significantly lower.

Even if you do not want to go through the learning curve of doing this yourself, there are relatively inexpensive ways of getting highly-skilled professionals to do it for you, as an outsourced service.

Again, the competitive and varied marketplace has forced prices down, and you may be amazed at how cheap some of these services are today. You just need to know the right places to look for them.

As devices to play and carry multimedia content along with you become more widely used, and as bandwidth costs come crashing down – while broadband Internet access is more widely accessible every day – the growth of demand for content presented in multimedia format is sure to become explosive. You, as an infopreneur, need to be positioned to take advantage of this demand, and meet it. Being informed about this coming wave is the first step. Getting ready is the next. And that one's up to you!

Where to Find Content?

There are four options:

• Create it yourself.
• Invite contributions.
• Hire content providers.
• Syndicate or license content from others.

Creating Your Own Content

Generating your own content for a website or information product is NOT easy!

If you have a lot of experience in your specialty, and your writing skills are excellent, content creation will be a simple matter of sitting at your computer and banging away at the keys for a few minutes or hours.

If, however, you aren't wired that way, crafting each segment of your information product will feel like having your teeth pulled out – without anesthetic !

But don't despair. Every problem has a simple solution. And after all, you have access to a global community of helpers via the Internet!

Before you decide to create your own content, you may want to consider these questions.

• Do you have the expertise? Are you really an expert? Can you write valuable, reliable, interesting content, and do it regularly? Most of your readers won't know much about your topic. But there will be the occasional expert. You can't fool your readers with pretense. Don't even try.

• Do you have the skills? Can you write well? You might understand General Relativity – but if you can't write clearly about it, Einstein himself might be confused!

• Do you have the time? Writing original content of a high quality can take a great deal of time – especially if your project is an ongoing thing like publishing an ezine or subscription magazine or membership website, week after week, issue after issue. Can you do it?

Inviting Contributions

If writing your own content is not suitable, don't despair. There are many people around who will be happy to write for your website.

Why would they do it?

Because writing for your website projects them as experts, and gives them exposure and access to your readers. Most often, all that these authors ask in return is a by-line: a short three-to-five-line description of the author and his/her business, at the end of an article or report.

So if you don't want to (or cannot) create your own content, ask others to help. Include a short note inviting articles from other authors in all your content. Then wade through the submissions and choose the best to present to your audience.

Contests - A Neat Content Idea

An interesting twist on this concept is to run an article-writing contest.

You can invite contributors to submit an article on a topic of your choice, for a chance to win a prize. You can also predetermine the title, word count, etc. You may offer a cash prize, or a free copy of one of your products or services.

Make sure you state clearly that all submissions become your property, to use in any way you like. That way, you'll get a flood of articles and other content forms you can use in your website or in a future information product.

Hire Content Providers

And then, there's the 'rich and lazy' way: pay someone else to create content for you!

Content providers come in different forms:

• Freelance authors are writers-on-contract, who will submit content on a pay-per-word or pay-per-article basis. You can use it any way you like.

• Full-time writers and content providers are employees who will provide professional-quality material for a regular salary.

If you (or your business) need the benefits of regularly-refreshed new content on your website, but you haven't the time or the necessary technical skills to keep up with it – you might consider the option of hiring a professional team to create that content. While this could turn out to be expensive, it might still be cheaper than trying to acquire the skills on your own.

Syndicate or License Content

Syndication is an interesting way to get high-quality content from experts at a reasonable cost.

In the syndication model, content created by an individual or a company is displayed on other partner blogs or websites, in return for a payment (flat fee or percentage of revenue generated) or some other form of compensation.

Licensing content for a specified period upon payment of a licensing fee is another option. For your website, you might consider syndicating or licensing content from:

• News services that provide brief updates and

news flashes on a variety of topics

• Content aggregators who collate information on a topic from around the Web

• Magazines and newspapers

• Content-rich niche portal sites

• Other websites on your topic.

Automated Content Systems

I know that some expert infopreneurs are reading this material in the hope of getting some fresh ideas. Although most of what we've talked about up to now is pretty much general knowledge, we're going to get into some more advanced stuff from here on in.

So in case you're just getting started, or lack the technical skills to carry out this part, don't worry. You'll still get an idea of what's possible, so that later on when you gain more experience with the process, you'll be able to take better advantage of these strategies.

Leveraging content to build multiple websites

Do not start writing an article or creating a form of content until you have first thought of at least three different ways to benefit from it. There are up to twenty ways you can re-purpose any form of content – and that's on the Internet alone! So, by thinking of three ways to use the content, you are barely scratching the surface of what's possible.

Here is a quick example to fire your imagination.

Let's say you've written (or bought) an article. Think of a strategy that will allow you to spin off multiple forms of content using this article.

An Easy Way: You could cut the article into pieces, and split it into a multi-page website.

A Slightly Complex Way: You could display it in different templates, creating a variety of web pages that look different from each other

Now extend this concept further, and you'll see how you can leverage content in a big way. If you know how to use some forms of programming like SSI (server side includes) or PHP, you can plan your website to be built as 'modules' of content.

For instance, you could have a header block, a content block (made up of articles or other content), a navigation block, and a page footer with relevant content. Of course, you could have even more 'module' blocks, if you wish.

Now, if you rotate blocks, or replace one module with a new one, you've got a brand new webpage! And the same content or article you wrote will be in it, multiplying your end result.

Just think about how powerful this can be!

And then, you can extend the same article to different display media, as we'll discuss in the next section. For example, an article on your website could become a post on your blog, an article submitted to

other directories or email newsletters, even published offline in a newspaper or magazine that your
target audience reads!

All these things leverage the time and effort you
spent in creating the article. By using them, you get
exponentially more power and effectiveness from
that one-time effort than you would from just publishing the article on your website.

Dynamically Inserting User-Created Content

Another way you can ensure your site grows organi-
cally with content you don't even have to write is to
work on a system to automatically incorporate content created by your visitors into your web pages.

A simple way to think about it is the electronic
'Guestbook'. When you host a 'Guestbook' on your
website, the comments your website visitors type
into a form are automatically added to your site.

For a moment, forget about the 'Guestbook' and
think about the concept.

How else can you get visitors to your site to post
something – an article, a comment, feedback, opinions or links to other useful resources – and have it
automatically included in your website's content?

Finished thinking? Great! You'll surely have come
up with these ideas – that already exist!

An Article Directory: Invite readers to submit an
article they wrote, which will go on your website
with a link to it from the directory. You could even

customize it using one of the article directory scripts (or have one programmed for you). This way, you can categorize them by author, subject, title, keyword, length, intended audience, and more.

Blog Comments: Even though it is now a much-abused feature of blogs, the ability to solicit and receive comments from readers is what makes blogs interactive and a powerful community-building tool. Spammers have wrecked this utility, just as they have email. But you can work around it by using various screening systems, such as requiring your comments to be moderated, or making the feature open only to registered members.

Feedback and Reviews: See Amazon.com's 'Book Review' feature. It's a great example of user feedback. You read a book, write a review, and it gets posted automatically to the relevant section of Amazon.com, after being moderated by an editor. (Oh, by the way, if you like this book, please pop over to Amazon. com and write a short review about it, won't you? Thanks.)

Opinions and Discussions: The same goes for software reviews on CNET.com. By asking readers to rate a product or service, and asking about the usefulness of such ratings to OTHER users, this could become a powerful way of encouraging addition of quality content to your website – effortlessly! Another spin to it can be setting up discussion forums on your niche topic, and then finding a way to 'feed' the most recent or especially interesting posts to the main page. Voilà! Instant, fresh, constantly-changing content.

Resource Links: While reciprocal link directories are frowned upon by many as primarily a sneaky way to build incoming links and boost popularity for your site, their primary reason for existence is to point visitors to other useful and helpful resources on a subject. And the directory listings themselves will become fodder for your content mill.

Newsmastering

Okay, now we're on a roll. Let's take this concept of automated content even higher – on to the exciting, cutting-edge specialty of 'Newsmastering'.

In the simplest sense, newsmastering is a technique where you automatically gather, sift through, and collate news and other content relevant to a specific, often very narrow, niche. You then present the collated information on your website in one or more of a variety of formats.

The beauty and elegance of the concept is that it runs on auto-pilot after it is set up correctly. The pain lies in the paucity of suitably powerful tools!

We're getting there, with web-based tools like RSS feed parsers and online search-enabled scripts scanning a vast range of news sources for the few nuggets of value. Frankly, this would be a task practically impossible to take on manually, not even counting the extraordinary time involvement. But the technology and tools are steadily improving and becoming more powerful, while simultaneously easier to use. This is sure to make newsmastering a very real skill that infopreneurs will want to acquire in the near future.

If you're thinking it's going to take a lot of time and effort to understand and master this area, you're right. But imagine how powerful it will be to have a system in place that goes out automatically, hunts down the best information on a subject or niche, and presents it on your site for your audience – and does it all while you're working on something else, or simply having fun! Being an auto-pilot infopreneur sure sounds attractive!

Customizing Content: Make Your Content Unique

The simplest way to make your content unique is to create it yourself!

If not that, have it created exclusively for you.

And then, protect it by copyrighting and do not give anyone else permission to use it, on pain of legal action.

Like all powerfully effective solutions, this one will take time, effort and money to put into action.

A quicker, easier way is to get your hands on content that already exists, and modify it to suit your needs.

Here's a question I've often heard asked about using 'reprint rights' or 'private label' articles:

"Will Google and other search engines view it as 'duplicate content' and penalize me for it? "

Well, yes... and no.

If you simply buy a pack of articles or pull them from a directory and slap them up on your website or submit them to article directories, your articles will be duplicates of others.

And that's the best reason NOT to use such articles in that way (apart from the ethical issues of copying other people's content, or feeding off someone else's work). Instead, spare a few moments and put in a little effort to make your articles unique. Here are a few easy ways you can do it:

Insert the articles into a unique website template.

Design (or have someone create) a unique website template for you. It acts as a container, and you'll slot your articles into a section of it where the rest of the template's content frames your article or content. This template doesn't have to be anything fancy (though it could be, if you're a good web designer). The very act of putting your content inside a template, framing it with other unique, related content, will distinguish it from all other content resources using the same article.

Of course, you'll have to make sure the 'frame' you're building around the 'borrowed' content is substantial enough to make a difference. For instance, if you put a 1,000-word article below an introductory paragraph that says:

"Here's a great article I just read about XXXX..."

... well, it probably won't make a big difference in the

content duplication score, since most of your content page will still be seen as identical to others.

Add an introductory paragraph to the article.

This is simple, elegant and effective.

Here's an example of an introductory paragraph I may use for some articles to which I buy private label rights:

§ § §

```
In this article, you will learn one of the
carefully-hidden secrets about_____ .
It's something many top experts know, and
every beginner would love to understand.
And it has the power to change the way you
think about this topic forever. Read it
very carefully.
```

§ § §

This has the dual benefit of both making my article unique, and also involving the reader in the consumption of the article, building up its value, enticing them to pay attention and read what follows.

You could write a unique introduction to each article you use on a content site. Or you could use a generic introduction like the one above. If you plan to go the second route, make sure you change a small part of it every now and then, or else that segment of text will become a 'fingerprint' by which SE's (and other people 'spying' on you) can quickly and easily locate all your published work. This is especially impor-

Think, Write and Retire

tant if you're playing in multiple niches, and don't want your competition to know exactly which ones they are!

Here are a few more ways you can make unique any generic content that you re-purpose for your use.

Delete at random around 30% of the article, or rewrite that 30%.

This is quick, easy, and relatively effective. If you have access to articles (private label or from other 'free to reprint' sources), you could simply delete a few sentences or paragraphs randomly, and get an end result that's unique to your site.

But make sure you read the article to see if it still makes sense and offers value to a human visitor to your website. Otherwise, what you're creating is little more than random sentences thrown together. If that's the extent of your goal, you will never become a true infopreneur.

Break up the article into several smaller sections of varying length.

I have used this technique in many different ways on my own websites. It is VERY effective.

Let's say you have a 5,000-word special report. You could split it up into 10 pages of 500 words each. Or 50 pages of 100 words each. Or any other combination. Best of all, your site will still retain value, even if you are forcing a reader to click on multiple links to complete reading your content.

Rearrange content in your article.

This is a tricky way to make your article unique, but it works!

All you do is juggle paragraphs around. For instance, take paragraph #1 and put it in the middle of the article; take another from the end and bump it up to the top; and if you're feeling particularly adventurous, repeat the process with other content!

However, once again, make sure the article is readable from the start to the end. There are more than enough scripts that take web content, slice and dice it up any way you like, and vomit out the result into a page of scrambled text that looks as if a monkey sat at your keyboard and banged on it!

If that kind of stuff makes you go "Wow! Cool!", then you're probably on a different wavelength. It all boils down to your 'content philosophy', which we'll be discussing next.

Modify or rewrite a section of the article in your own words.

Now we're getting into a more advanced form of content modification, one where you practically co-author the piece. You add value to the outline you're starting out with, throwing in your opinions, comments, improvements, reviews or more. You could go to any extent with this, even practically rewriting the article in your own words, thus making it entirely unique.

All of these techniques are quick and easy to follow.

Any of them will set your version of the article collection apart from any other on the web. To save yourself time and trouble, you could even hire someone to help you with it.

Your Content Philosophy

Maybe this sounds like hocus-pocus, but I believe it is critical to your success or failure as an information marketer. So please bear with me and read this section carefully.

There's a lot of confusion and controversy about fair, ethical use of articles and other forms of content on the Internet. They apply particularly to content that you haven't created yourself.

Broadly, in content marketing (just as in life itself) there are two categories of people:

• those who exploit a situation, and
• those who make the world a better place.

Now, I'm not getting into a debate or discourse on which is better, holier, or more 'right'. Which path you opt to tread is entirely your choice, and might depend upon factors I don't know and cannot imagine. Just understand that there are two distinct paths.

Those who exploit the prevailing content-marketing scenario are focused on one thing, and that alone. They want to obtain a high ranking on search engines for competitive keywords (ones that offer multiple quick ways to make money from visitors) and drive floods of traffic to their sites... never mind how they do it.

And there are many 'black hat' tactics to achieve this end . They can use scripts and software, ingeniously mixed together, to throw up 'junk content sites' that often make very little sense, purposely look ugly or repulsive, and are geared to doing one thing well: getting visitors to click on money-spinning links that are placed on these websites.

I have little experience with this style of content marketing, but I know it is profitable. During the heyday of Google Adsense – a contextual advertising program launched by the search engine giant, Google.com – many folks were banking five-figure checks every month, based on this kind of strategy.

Here's the downside: these sites may not last for long in search engines. When Google realized that the black-hat techniques being used by some content publishers were adversely affecting the experience their service was delivering to the search users, they cracked down heavily on the 'junk content' sites. Big checks magically vaporized into thin air.

The owners of this type of content sites will always be scrambling to stay ahead of the game. If you decide to follow them, you shouldn't mind if you too lose your cash-generating high-traffic magnets overnight. Just keep building some more. And then more. If this sounds like working for money, you're right. It is. Don't confuse this with a real 'infopreneur business'.

Sure, you'll make money – maybe a lot of it. But you don't have a sustained process for acquiring clients, making repeat sales to them, building a list, and achieving steady growth across a longer time frame. That approach, by the way, is at the core of a successful, sustainable infopreneur business.

The other category of people is the ones who want to 'make the Internet a better place'. They do this by adding valuable content to the Web.

While this is a harder path to tread, in the longer term it is more sustainable and can be scaled up over time. There's some hard work involved while things get going, but after a while it can be organized to be 'set-and-forget' simple.

There are some content sites I built in 1999, and haven't touched since then except for renewing the domain names. Even today, these sites get hundreds or even thousands of visitors every month; and they bring in a few hundred dollars in profit each month, hands-free.

That's the difference. With this strategy, in the end the result is a high-quality, content-rich website. This site is a useful online resource many people visit over and over again, because it truly adds value to their lives in some way. It's a place people tell other people to go for quality information and support.It's a portal that search engines will find and reward, sooner or later. It's even a website that could become an authority on the niche topic around which it is built.

This kind of site will easily be able to create a sense of online community among users, nurture a loyal following and have staying power. And this can become the kernel for a business built around that theme.

Which model do you want to follow?

As I said before, it's your choice to make. Both are lucrative models. Both need some work. They have some significant operational and strategic differences. Most important, they are philosophically distinct.

Your choice of one over the other is a reflection of your own attitude and approach towards your online business. Just make sure you're clear about which kind you're going after, since much of what you'll do in the weeks ahead will be determined by this decision.

How to Show Off:
Packaging Your Expertise for Maximum Impact

Let's quickly recap what you've learned until now. You have reviewed things you know, things about which you can justifiably claim 'expert' status. You have identified the correct audience – people who want that information and are willing to pay for it. You have thought out the best format for sharing that information.

Once you have your content written or recorded, the next big decision you'll have to make as an infopreneur is how best to package and present it to your audience for maximum reach and impact.

We'll take a look at the multiple forms in which your information product can be presented, so that every kind of potential audience can find it in a style best suited to their needs.

Books and eBooks

If you have meaty, long, categorized content about a particular subject, you could make it a complete book (like this one you're reading). Break down the material into chapters, each chapter covering one aspect of the information you are sharing. Then compile it into a book for publication.

You may either have it printed and sell it as a book, or deliver it as an electronic counterpart called an e-book. A book can be sold in bookstores, in person, via postal order, at special events, bundled with other products, through associations and industry groups, and in a myriad of other ways. You can either have it published by a major publishing house (with its own unique process), or self-publish and market it yourself.

An e-book would be delivered digitally over the Internet, at no shipping or handling expense. You also save money on publishing it or storing inventory. The cost saving goes right into your bottom-line profit. This is why many infopreneurs begin their exciting venture into the information product market by writing an e-book.

Audio Books

The audio book market is already around $2 billion a year, and the trend towards downloads is becoming stronger by the day. MP3 players are everywhere; downloadable audio books are selling faster than ever. The frontrunner in retailing audio books is Audible.com (now a subsidiary of online book selling giant, Amazon.com), and they had sales of $63.07 million in 2005. In 2006, they reached that figure in six months. In other words, their sales doubled and they were already very big.

With the advent of the ubiquitous iPod, and constantly-evolving partnerships between innovative publishing houses and businesses that control access to their audience, this trend is only going to accelerate and grow bigger over time. Positioning yourself to take advantage of this situation might be one of the smartest decisions you'll make as an infopreneur.

Presenting your book in the form of audio is now

simple and inexpensive. You can offer it for download, streaming audio delivery over the Internet; or you can deliver your book in physical format, burned onto CD, DVD, or audio tapes. Gone are the days when you needed to hire or buy complex equipment or had to rent space in a recording studio.

Today, you can have a professional voice-over recording service convert your text content into high-quality audio for an affordable price. Shop around: you'll be surprised how low prices can be. And now it's possible to convert your home computer into a multimedia digital recording studio that will rival the best. You can use the software that comes bundled with your computer, or purchase it for a few hundred dollars; and your hardware is of a quality that – just a decade ago – was only accessible to professional audio creators.

While file size for downloadable audio can be large, and bandwidth cost to distribute it can add up, delivering audio content over the Internet is still cheaper than making it available in physical product form. To meet the demand, services like Amazon.com S3 have emerged, which let you distribute huge files at affordable cost. The future of digital audio and video looks rosy, that's for sure!

Audio Programs and Cassettes

You can also deliver complete training programs as audio information products by putting them on CD, DVD, tapes, or sharing them on the Internet as streaming audio. The material you distribute as audio could be the actual course content, or just a sampler that serves as sales copy for the full program.

Marketing expert Jay Abraham sends out a single
cassette tape of an interview he did with motivation-
al guru Tony Robbins. That hour-long conversation
contains powerful tips that showcase Jay's expertise.
After listening to that tape, and seeing how effective
were the concepts he taught, I have since bought
over $7,500 worth of his training material! That's
how influential an audio program can be as a marketing vehicle.

Video Presentations

With sophisticated and highly-capable video recording equipment becoming more widely available and
progressively less expensive, audio-visual recordings
are becoming a very common mode of presenting
information products. YouTube.com revolutionized
the concept of disseminating content across the Web
in video format, offering its service to video makers
for free.

Suddenly, home-video creators could access massive
audiences all over the world. There are many videos
on YouTube that have been viewed over a million
times! And that trend appears to be gaining even
more popularity, with the mushrooming of social networking sites that share video virally among their
users.

The viewing devices have also grown in choice and
versatility. Today you can watch multimedia presentations and digital video recordings on your TV, computer, cell phone, handheld PDA or Blackberry, and
on your iPod or iPhone. Wireless technology allows

this content to be conveniently and widely streamed over the Internet. Bandwidth costs are low enough to make this content distribution channel financially viable to publishers.

With conversion devices that allow interlinking of computers to TV, streamed video content can be conveniently downloaded on a computer. It can then be viewed on TV, enhancing the experience and making it more 'familiar' to viewers. Innovation in this area is constant, fast, and furious. By the time you read this book, something exciting and new may have entered the market and changed the game – again!

Workbooks

For more intense coaching programs that are narrowly focused on a specific subject or sub-topic, a workbook might be the optimal choice of delivering an information product. Workbooks allow the learner to move along a pre-structured path, step by step, with tips and guidance being provided at every stage.

Assignments or self-evaluation checklists incorporated into the workbook allow progress to be measured and compared against others following the same program. The finished workbook remains a useful revision tool when the student wants to refresh her memory on specific elements.

Group Coaching, Apprenticeships, and Mentoring

When you expand your thinking about information products to embrace the delivery of information to the target audience in multiple ways, it becomes obvious that coaching, apprenticeship, and mentoring programs can also be viewed as 'information products'.

Group coaching can be done in person, by means of teleconferences, or virtual networking over the Internet. "Webinars," or web seminars, are an interesting format of delivery, as are virtual classrooms.

These save time and money, both for program organizers and attendees. The course can be tailored to be accessible from home and at a time convenient to both sides. With travel costs soaring, this lets you, as an infopreneur, justify charging more money for your training – because you're providing it conveniently, right from the student's home computer. Recordings can even be made available to registered members, further extending the benefit and value to the learner.

Public Speaking

Lectures delivered on a very specific topic are one more vehicle of disseminating your information product. Keynote addresses, presentations at seminars and workshops, boot camps for a small group of students, and other forms of platform speaking are all interesting methods of delivering an information product.

Speaking in public can involve many different approaches. You could be delivering a presentation or research paper or case study at an industry convention or conference. You might conduct educational or informational public seminars to increase awareness about the topic of your information product. In this case, you can set things up so that some members of your audience get excited, nervous, or curious enough to want more detailed information – and buy one of your infoproducts on the subject.

Corporate Training

This form of infoproduct sales can be very lucrative, especially when the information is specialized, valuable, and can be systematized and applied to diverse industries. A friend of mine spent years evolving a specialized program that could be used to train people in a particular skill. The program was deemed of great value by the U.S. government, which licensed this content for a training program in the Department of Defense. This earned my friend a royalty of several million dollars every year!

Industry-specific programs that can be easily adapted to similar companies on a nationwide, or even International scale, can become the seed of a great fortune. Information products can be scaled up to any level you wish; and since you are an infopreneur, your imagination is the only limiting factor to how big you want to become.

Boot Camps

These are short (two-to-five-day) events for small, select groups of participants. An expert or coach teaches intricate nuances of a niche topic, covering all angles. It is a quick, though intense, way for participants to gain information and expertise in an area.

A boot camp can also be a follow-up information product, offered to buyers of a book or audio-video training program. It could be one of a sequence of increasingly higher-priced products offered in your catalog, to take a prospect through growing levels of value related to the information you share.

Consulting

The most valuable form of infopreneuring is 'real time' use of your brain-power – as a consultant. This is also often the most expensive version, because you are really exchanging time for money, and the price you charge should make it worth your while.

Consulting lets you tailor the delivery of information to the needs of your client. You might offer different versions of consulting. A time-denominated contract, like hourly or daily consulting, is suitable for some circumstances. A longer-term consulting contract might be better for both you and the client in other situations.

You may even try 'subscription consulting' where your clients pick the duration or package most likely to meet their needs. The attractiveness of this model is that it can be renewed or extended for as long as required, by paying extra.

For most forms of consulting-style information marketing, it helps to have a solid introductory-level product like a book or cassette recording that will give your prospective consulting client an idea of your depth of experience and skills in teaching your specialty. Once the lead-in product establishes your credentials as an expert, the most highly-motivated

readers who want personalized help with growing their knowledge in your field of interest will
gravitate towards becoming your consulting clients.
They'll be happy to pay you higher fees for highly-
personalized, intensive, specific, and even confiden-
tial information.

Licensing and Syndication

A highly-leveraged form of information marketing,
licensing and syndication take advantage of already-
existing content delivery channels being used to
reach audiences that would be otherwise difficult to
access. You can tap into these channels and showcase
your information product to a broad new audience.
The licensing agency either pays a fee or offers extra exposure as an incentive to using their services,
which benefit you as an infopreneur by extending
your brand visibility.

Licensing or syndicating your content to other services and businesses for their own use, in exchange for
a fee or share of revenues generated, is itself a profit
model for your information product business.

Home Study Courses

If you conduct boot camps and seminars that require
participants to come to your program venue, then by
recording, transcribing, and compiling what goes on
at these events, you'll have another instant information product. Use this to take the program to a different audience – those who couldn't make it to the
actual seminar, for example – thus vastly expanding
your product's reach.

A home study course is immensely valuable to busy
or housebound prospects who cannot (or will not)
make the extra effort of coming to a live event.
These customers can get all the benefit of your content (without the in-person networking benefits)
simply from your home study version. You can price
this form of your information product on par with
your seminar or boot camp, maybe even higher – and
boost your profit from information marketing.

What is often surprising to many infopreneurs is the
fact that attendees of a live session (seminar, boot
camp, or coaching program) will often also purchase
a home study version, even though it means paying
extra. The home study version lets them review and
revise sections of these intense sessions over and over,
obtaining even greater value from the information.

Newsletters and Ezines

Another simple, effective, and very popular method
of information product selling is in the form of a
newsletter in physical or digital format (ezine). Your
newsletters may be free publications that pre-sell a
more expensive version of in-depth content. In this
case, the newsletter provides enough value to convince a reader about the credentials and expertise of
you, the author.

On the other hand, the newsletter or ezine itself may
be a product, for which subscribers pay on a periodic
basis, or with a single lifetime access fee. There is
nothing, however, to prevent using a paid newsletter
in the same way as a free one, to lead a prospective
buyer into purchasing more expensive, elaborate,

higher-value products or services related to the subject matter of your publication.

Newsletters are typically shorter than books or special reports. They often contain one or two feature articles, some news updates, event listings, industry trends, and other relevant information to readers interested in the niche being covered.

Radio and TV Shows

An extension of the presentation of content in audio and video format is to tailor it for vast viewership through radio or TV. In most cases, the use of these media by infopreneurs is determined by level of aggressiveness in promoting their information product.

The radio or TV show can be modestly informative, especially if conducted in the form of an interview. This can again showcase your expertise, making a viewer more likely to purchase a more advanced, expensive form of your information product in the future.

A unique twist to doing a radio or TV show is the 'infomercial'. This is an informative commercial that usually airs in non-prime time slots, and sells your product or service in the context of providing informative content related to it. This can be quite expensive, and requires access to some specialized resources and expertise.

Private Label Content

Another interesting way to extend the reach of your content and information is to allow others to label it as their own content!

In a sense, this works like syndicating your content, except that the person using your content is granted permission to edit, modify, add on to, and even completely claim ownership of your information product.

On the face of it, this appears to be destroying your potential as an infopreneur. But when you think about it deeply, it is a clever way to break into a wider market than you might manage on your own. If you are an excellent information product creator but not so hot as a marketer, you could ensure wide distribution of your information by aligning with good marketers and offering them private label rights to your content.

Another way to leverage private label rights is by including references to your core business or product within your information product. By doing this, if the person exercising private label rights chooses to leave those references intact, the information product serves to raise awareness about your business or related products and services -- to a wide audience.

Ghostwriting

In a very similar fashion to private label rights, you could partner with other marketers or business owners and be a ghostwriter for them, profiting from creating information they will use in their business. In the private label rights model, you first create the information product and then offer it to others for them to use. With the ghostwriting model, you are hired to create an information product according to specifications decided by the person or business contracting with you.

Co-Authoring

If you are not an excellent writer, but have knowledge and core expertise to share in your topic or subject area, you could partner with a recognized writer and enter into a co-authoring arrangement. This would also work if you join forces with another writer to create a joint project which spans different areas in which each of you is an expert. The collaborative effort may be more valuable to your readers than anything either of you could create on your own.

Special Reports and White Papers

If you have very specialized information on a narrow niche topic, you could present it in the form of a special report or white paper, instead of a full-blown book or ebook.

This is particularly useful for shorter reports of five to 50 pages that are timely or seasonal, include industry-specific information, and have content that is directly useful to buyers who will often be able to put the knowledge to use quickly and reap huge profits.

Some examples are a stock-picking tip sheet, or a betting sheet suggesting favorites for each race; or, on the higher end, a detailed analysis of online shopping and ecommerce trends during the Christmas season, or the future of global oil prices in the next three months. All of these are infoproducts that will provide value to their target audiences, who, in turn, will willingly pay for access to this information.

Mini-Books

These are essentially condensed or abridged versions
of your full book, and are often used as premium content. They cover most of the issues in the book, but
do not go into great detail about specifics. By saving
time spent on reading and cutting right to the chase,
mini-books are sometimes perceived as higher value
than longer books. And, after all, the regular book is
always available as a reference guide, should further
information become necessary.

Directories and Resource Guides

A form of information product that is not often considered by infopreneurs, but can be immensely valuable for specific topics and subjects, is a directory or
resource compilation. The Yellow Pages is one such
example, as is the phone book.

A directory or resource guide can be the ideal form
of presenting valuable information to certain audiences. For a new tenant or person moving into a
neighborhood, a guide to the area will offer details
like shopping spots, furniture and carpeting stores,
gardening, plumbing, carpentering and electrical
services, clubs and recreation spots – in short, the
kind of data a new resident would need, but find
hard to collect by himself. An orientation manual for
new employees joining an organization can shorten
time taken to settle down, improve efficiency, and
lead to better employee morale.

Software

This is a complete world of information products with a vast range and depth. Information products in the form of software could be standalone software that one installs onto computers, PDAs, mobile phones, or other devices. They could be presented as off-the-shelf solutions or custom-programmed scripts for specific uses.

Software could also be Internet-based, requiring the user to log on to a website to access the features provided. Templates used for a variety of purposes like drafting business letters, creating websites, crafting legal documents or contracts for joint ventures can all be presented as software.

Business-Building Systems

Your information product may take the form of a course or systems training. It may showcase a particular set of processes that can be exported to other industries, or other locations in the same industry. When implemented, these systems bring about significant improvement in efficiency and/or profit. The information product is presented in a series of steps or actions to be taken, which the buyer or licensee then implements step by step in her business or organization.

This kind of information product can be tailored to fit many different niches. It could show service professionals (doctors, dentists, chiropractors, fitness coaches, sports trainers, and more) how to grow a practice and attract more clients, becoming a practice-building system. Or it can teach real estate agents, door-to-door salespeople and telemarketers how to sell more effectively. Or it can show restaurant owners, movie theater managers and event organizers how to get more seats filled.

The presentation of the systems training will need to be suitably adapted to meet the needs of each audience. It can be presented in written form, or as audio training or video demonstrations.

Seminars

Sharing your information in the form of a presentation or live interaction at seminars and workshops is still another way to distribute your content. You may conduct seminars yourself and share your information with attendees, either for free or for a fee. You could even develop content specifically for use by others, and license them for presentation by other speakers at seminars.

Home Education

Guides designed to train adults or offer home-schooling solutions can become one more avenue by which infopreneurs can expand their market reach. Your information product may need to be repackaged in the form of lessons or chapters, and presented in smaller portions to be studied and understood before moving ahead to the next stage. By incorporating self-assessment questionnaires, or even formal surveys or tests on the portion studied, your material can become a complete course designed to teach adults or home-schoolers specific subjects or topics.

Blogs and Podcasts

One of my early infoproducts was delivered in the form of a web log (or blog). It was presented in the form of a day-by-day set of posts, outlining methods of profiting from blogging. In all, there were 33 techniques, which were posted to the blog daily for a month, and made accessible only to paying customers.

Podcasting is the technique of posting audio messages to a blog. More recently, Vlogging (using video in blog posts) has caught the attention of many bloggers. Both these multimedia blogging modalities offer other formats of content presentation for infopreneurs.

Which format is best? What should you use?

There's an advantage in implementing a strategy that presents your information product in as many of these formats as feasible. With each additional 'channel', you will gain access to a completely new universe of prospects, people who might not sample or buy your infoproduct if it had not been available in their preferred fashion.

If you choose only to publish a book, you will reach a segment of your potential market that visits bookstores, prefers information in the form of words and pictures, and has developed the reading habit. But with leisure time becoming scarce, and more interest being captured by multimedia devices like the television, computer, and mobile computing instruments, the number of book readers is static, even dropping. (In a 2006 survey, only 38% of adults said they had spent time reading a book for pleasure the previous day, and 65% of college freshmen in 2005 said they read little or nothing for pleasure.)

(Reference: http://www.parapublishing.com/sites/para/resources/statistics.cfm)

But if you implement alternative delivery channels for your information product, you have a better chance of reaching a group of readers who may not have bought your book, but will consume the information because it is available to them in a format they prefer.

So go through the list we just discussed, and jot down notes about the ones you can start using first. Then, as your information empire grows and expands, you can include more of them, fuelling explosive growth by reaching a wider audience.

Show Me The Money!
Your Infopreneuring Profit Models

Despite all the apparent complexity and diversity of multiple streams of profit from infopreneuring, it can all be distilled down to three core profit models. Let's take a look at the three models and see if that can help you decide what suits you best.

Begin With Your Purpose

I believe a lot depends on your purpose. It's the defining force, in my mind, for what anyone does in their infopreneur business – or indeed, anything at all.

Your "Why" determines, more than anything else, your success at content marketing. It drives you to keep going, gives you the energy and enthusiasm to stick with it despite hurdles and setbacks, and fulfills you deeply when you achieve success.

Spend some time thinking about it before you begin. Are you in this to make some extra cash? Is it going to be your sole income earner? Will it complement something else you're working on? Is it the first step in a bigger plan?

Also, think about the deeper reason you do what you do. If you want to replace your day job, think of it as a way to spend more time at home, with your family or doing what you like, rather than punching a clock and doing the 9-to-5 grind. If you're looking for supplemental income, focus on what you want to do with it: take a vacation, indulge in a small luxury,

get your kids something special, buy yourself a new
car or home – whatever.

What's all this got to do with being an infopreneur?
In a word: Everything!

It's absolutely critical that you get the right mindset.
And that's the attitude that says you're going to win,
no matter what.

If you think this attitude is going to appear magically out of nowhere, think again. It takes time
and patience, and a lot of introspection and thought
about your priorities.

When you come home tired from work, are you going
to crash in front of the TV? Or will you sit down in
front of your computer and update your website?

When you're feeling depressed and frustrated, are
you going to wallow in your misery? Or will you force
yourself to crank out that next article?

When you're constantly 'failing' after trying one
thing after another, when nothing seems to work, are
you going to throw up your hands and say "Enough,"
and quit? Or will you keep trying the next one, and
the next, and yet another ... until you crack the code?

All of these choices hinge on your purpose – and your
passion.

After repeated requests, I once posted to my blog
about a typical day in my life. It might sound crazy
and hectic. It's both. It's also what I'm passionate
about. Find your true inner driving force for your

infopreneuring effort and you can't help succeeding. You'll attract success with your attitude and effort.

The Three Models of Infopreneuring

Things are complex; yet, at their core, they are simple. And at a very basic level, there are only three 'models' infopreneurs use.

1. Direct Selling;

2. Content Publishing; and

3. Lead Generating.

Direct Selling involves, as the name suggests:

• creating an information product,
• writing a sales letter to share it with others in exchange for a payment,
• convincing a prospect that your offer is worth accepting; and finally,
• completing the transaction.

'Selling' doesn't have to involve only products. It could be a subscription to your list, a registration to your coaching program, a decision to call your toll-free number or drive up to your store or mail in a rebate coupon.

If your online business aims to 'sell' a product or service, your desired end point is to get the order. If it aims to 'sell' a subscription, your goal is to get a prospect to sign up to your mailing list. If it strives to convince a visitor to make a decision, success is measured by how many of them actually make it.

Content Publishing

Content publishing is the second model. As we saw in an earlier chapter, 'Content' is defined as much more than simply words on a web page. Content is anything that you make available for consumption by a visitor to your website, a subscriber to your magazine or podcast or TV show, an attendee at your live event.

Articles are content. So are graphics, video, audio, and other forms of multimedia. Software, scripts, and applications are content too. And in this model, the content becomes a driver that pulls prospects into your vortex, so you can work out methods and systems to monetize them.

Lead Generating

Lead generating is the third model. Here, the info-preneur focuses entirely upon getting targeted prospects to raise their hands and identify themselves as being interested in something: a book, a vacation spot, a hobby, an asset class, a kind of outcome, anything.

Variations on the theme involve incentives handed out to get the right prospects to respond, and follow-up processes that enhance conversion of a 'warm' prospect into a red-hot customer. These leads are worked, sold, rented or brokered out for a profit.

Almost every kind of online infopreneuring model fits into one (or sometimes a combination) of these three basic models. There probably are a few others, but these three versions account for the great majority. And since you are a student of the subject, these are the areas you need to be concerned with, analyze, and use to plan your own business strategically.

Choosing Your Business 'Model'

One thing that annoys me no end is how people with little or no experience in an area try and teach others about it!

Personally, I have no experience at all with the 'Lead Generation' model of online business. Sure, I can teach you how to get leads; I've learned a lot about it. But I wouldn't have the faintest clue about how to turn these leads into a source of profit (except in my own business, which is based on the other two models). That's why I do not teach it.

As for the other two models – direct selling and content publishing – I have explored them in many different ways, and have a vast storehouse of tested and proven methods, some of which I'll share with you.

The Direct Selling Model: An Outline

As we briefly discussed earlier, the 'direct selling' model aims to convince a prospect to take a specific course of action. It could be making a purchase. It could be signing up for a list. It could be making a phone call. It could be anything else.

At its core, this model is based upon using persuasive arguments to convince a prospect that doing what you want him to do is in the prospect's best interests. This means using copywriting and sales skills to influence a prospect's thinking.

As an Internet infopreneur looking to pursue this direct selling model, there are two major things you require:

• Traffic . As many pre-qualified, targeted, interested visitors as possible should visit your sales website, so that they can learn more about your information product, and buy it.

• Conversion. Your sales letter or webpage should make a compelling case to convince prospects that buying your information product right away is their best choice. Powerful, effective, informative copywriting is a skill that will serve you very well as an infopreneur. But there are many other variables that have an impact on the sales conversion of a website.

Now, on the face of it, this may appear simplistic. But there are many instances of how a struggling infopreneur neglected one or both of these critical factors – and failed, even with an excellent product or service.

For example, take the case of a video called 'Numa, numa' which caught the fancy of an online audience when it first was shown on YouTube.com Almost TWO MILLION people watched that funny video. But the product creator didn't make a cent. Why not? Because his 'sales page' did not convert. It didn't get viewers to join a mailing list for more funny videos. There was no relevant product or service to sell on the back of this popularity.

It must have felt nice, for a while. But in the end, there was no profit to be made.

In comparison to conversion, traffic is relatively easier to get. You can buy it online, from pay-per-click services like Google Adwords (though cost is a limiting factor), or others like it. Or you can borrow it from other sites that have the traffic, by running advertisements on them, sending out email marketing messages to their mailing lists, or even getting other websites to sell you part of their traffic on a regular basis.

Finally, you can create your own traffic by using search engine optimization skills, publishing a blog, posting on forums, writing and distributing articles, and sending out press releases.

Even though the direct selling model appears more complex than others, it is perhaps the best, most lucrative, and scalable of the three infopreneur business models. By acquiring or building a client database, you sow the seeds of a long-term business that will grow on the foundation of a loyal customer base. By progressively selling these buyers more extensive, specialized, or valuable material, you can grow profits exponentially, at very little added cost, because you will be marketing to an already-existing client group.

The ways to profit from such a model are many. You could sell an information product or service. It could be your own, or something created by a partner whom you promote as an affiliate, in exchange for a share of the profit or a flat referral fee. You could use this initial sale to build a mailing list, and mar-

ket to those on the list over time. You could attract
prospects into any other kind of marketing process,
so they get exposed to your other information products over time, and hopefully convert into paying
customers over the long term.

This direct selling model can involve online marketing, offline marketing, or a combination of both.
Writing a powerful sales letter that makes an attractive offer is the cornerstone of success in this model.

The Content Publishing Model: An Overview

The content publishing model is very similar to
traditional print media. It is an attractive option for
infopreneurs who are not interested in selling stuff
to prospects (or managing the other mandatory steps
that are necessary, like delivering product, handling
customer support, and trouble-shooting problems,
not to mention following up to sell more).

You, the infopreneur, publish valuable content
around a specific theme. Attract viewers based upon
the quality of the content being provided. Then monetize their visits in one of many ways.

You can do this on the Internet using various techniques. Contextual ads placed around or within
content are useful. They can generate income from
advertisers who are willing to pay you for the chance
to place their ads in front of targeted audiences who
may be interested in their offers.

Pay-to-access services charge readers to read or listen to the content. Some publishers use the content-

syndication model, where other providers pay the creator to use their unique content. Packaging the content into ebooks, reports, membership sites, and other formats is another option.

And there are even more ways to do it offline – though it is more expensive than the online version. You could become a featured columnist in a magazine, or a syndicated or freelance reporter for a periodical or newspaper.

You could sell the content to businesses that might be able to use it in advertising brochures, educational manuals for their prospects, material for their trade newsletter or industry magazine, and in many other ways.

The model thrives on the value and uniqueness of the content, which in turn gets the websites ranked higher on search engines, attracting targeted visitors to the website. Your content also pre-sells prospects so that they are more positively inclined to doing business with the company, after getting valuable information and education from you first.

If you use the material as content for your website and keep it valuable, fresh, and frequently updated, you will get visitors to come back frequently to your site. This model is capable of generating self-sustaining income over time.

More important than the nuts-and-bolts details is the concept that I want you to grasp. These 'soft issues' are what takes years of hard-earned experience to gain and act upon.

The Lead Generation Model

Lead generation is based on the knowledge that there are companies and businesses eagerly seeking the kind of audience that is already out there, looking for the information you are sharing; and that these businesses are willing to pay you to help them find it.

You have set the bait on your website, which is useful, helpful, valuable content – a lot of it. This attracts a specific audience with targeted interests, people who spend time on your website consuming your information. As they do so, you present them with relevant offers. You encourage them to share their contact details, preferences, and requirements with those companies or businesses. The implied promise is that the businesses can help your prospects reach whatever goal they seek, or solve whatever problem they want taken care of.

By collecting the demographic details of these visitors, by inviting them to respond to surveys, or to fill in an online form, you are in the enviable position of being able to profit from your audience without having to sell anything. The better qualified a lead, and the more relevant data you are able to present to the businesses that buy your leads, the higher price you can command for them.

There are many nuances to implementing these three basic models to monetize your information. If you want more detailed information about them, you can check out the home study course for Internet Infopreneurs at. http://internetinfopreneur.com

But How Will People Know About You?
Your 30-Day Marketing Blueprint

As an Internet infopreneur, your most powerful competitive advantage stems from being able to drive a high volume of interested prospects to your web page, or otherwise get your marketing message in front of as many targeted eyeballs as possible.

This book is not a marketing manual. If it was, it would be twice as long; and even then it wouldn't begin to scratch the surface of what is possible. To keep it tightly themed on the subject of learning to become an Internet infopreneur, I will stick to a simple, yet effective plan to promote your website on the Internet and bring more visitors to your home on the Web.

Not surprisingly, the marketing methods in this section will be mainly about promoting your website online. But there are many more excellent, effective, economical marketing techniques you can use offline, to drive visitors to your website.

30 Days to More Website Traffic

This is a no-fluff guide to driving more traffic to your website in 30 days. Your daily lessons will be short, to the point, and sometimes even cryptic.

If you wish to seek clarification about any of the traffic methods discussed in the course, please join the "Think, Write and RETIRE!" tribe and visit the forum where we discuss the nuances of this blueprint. Someone there may be able to answer your question.

Reading through this chapter without taking action along the way will be a waste of time. I hope you will not let that happen, but use it as a roadmap to plan and execute an action program that will attract a flood of visitors to your content-rich infopreneur website. Get ready to work hard for 30 days – and enjoy the rich rewards of your effort for many years to come!

BLOGGING

If you don't have a blog (or 'web log') yet, set one up. WordPress and Movable Type are excellent blog programs. Blogger (at http://www.Blogger.com) is the quickest to get started without struggling with technical issues. Which platform you pick to use for blogging is up to you. But get your blog set up right away. This will become one of your most powerful traffic-driving methods, so don't delay it.

How to set up your Blogger.com blog

First, go to http://www.Blogger.com. If this is your first time there, take a few minutes to look around, study the tutorials and take the quick tour. It will give you a nice overview of the service and you'll get a fair idea about how to create your own blog. Then, register for an account and enter all the relevant data.

You'll have to choose a blog title and your preferred blog address. Make sure that both your title and blog URL (web address) contain a term or keyword related to the subject of your information product.

Choose your template from the selection offered by
the service. Then make your first post; just a short
test message will do.

Customize your blog so it is optimized for your best
keywords. This involves making minor changes to
the description, labels, and other elements of the
template. If you are not familiar with this process,
you can hire someone to do it for you, or find a free-
lancer who'll help you get this done.

Next, do these three things:

• Label your blog's 'Categories' as your top five niche
keywords. Hopefully, you have already done some
keyword research and identified the terms most of
your target audience are using to find information on
the Internet.

• Modify the blog templates. Replace words like
'Trackback', 'Permalink' and 'Comments' to include
your top keywords in every post.

• With every post you make, include your keyword
in the TITLE of your blog post in addition to a short,
catchy description about the content that follows.
Remember, this title will be what most prospects will
see first, and use to decide whether or not to explore
your blog in greater depth.

In addition to basic optimization of your blog, there
are two more things to modify:

• Include a list of services to 'ping' (announce updates as soon as they are made) in the box that allows you to ping directories automatically, every time

you post to your blog. (If you don't understand what this means, do some online research into pinging and RPC codes for pinging services. Each blog platform has a different way to set up automatic pinging: read the instructions for your choice of blog program.

• Go to 'Socializer' - http://www.ekstreme.com/socializer/ - and set up an account. Pick up the code that is generated automatically for your blog, and include it in every blog post. This will make it easy for readers to bookmark your blog, and increase the chances of others stumbling across it, thus bringing in more visitors.

Also, make sure that you include links to your main website within your template, so that the blog will drive traffic back to your main website. This, of course, includes a sales page for your information product. Finally, if you want to keep track of your traffic, set up a web statistics program like Google Analytics on your blog.

While this does sound like hard work, you only have to do it once, and then you'll enjoy the benefits for months, if not years. After all this is done, it is time to make your first post to the blog.

What to blog about

Anything related to the subject of your information product. A good system is to sign up for a service provided by Google called 'Google Alerts', which will deliver email notifications of breaking news and newly-listed websites related to your niche. These email alerts will depend upon the keywords or topics you choose while setting up your account.

You can then open an email notification, click on the links in it to visit the news story, read it, and think of a short comment or opinion about it. Type out a short post (50 to 100 words), copy a short excerpt of the news story, and paste it beneath your comment, with a link to the full story in case readers want to learn more.

Even though it may appear that the link off your website might take visitors away, in reality, it enhances your visitor's experience. It also increases the chances they will come back to your blog later. Even search engines reward this practice of linking to related, relevant sites. Best of all, over time you'll be viewed as an authority on your niche topic!

Try to aim for three blog posts every day, starting right from the first day. For best results, keep your posts at least 30 minutes apart from each other.

If you have been blogging three times every day, after a week you should have around 10 to 15 posts on your blog. That's enough to begin submitting it to specialized blog directories. Make as many of these submissions as possible. There are many different lists of directories. If this will take too much time, outsource it to someone, but get it done. As your blog grows in content, the directories will drive more traffic to it – so the sooner you begin, the better.

Your blog automatically generates a piece of code called an RSS feed. This allows easy syndication of your blog content to other websites, and lets 'subscribers' to your blog read it conveniently on their computer desktops in a program called a 'feed reader'.

The quickest, easiest way to extend the reach of your
feed is to submit it to various RSS feed directories.
There are hundreds of them – but don't let that put
you off. Start submitting today, and keep going for as
many days as it takes to get your feed listed in many
places. Automated software to help you do this is
also available.

Using Technorati Tags

Technorati tags are a system for categorizing your
blog content by associating it with relevant keywords
matching the content of your blog. This is a powerful
marketing tactic for your blog, bringing you inbound
links from an authority site as well as some targeted
traffic.

Paste your Technorati tags to the end of every blog
post you make, and then ping Technorati to let them
know you've updated it (this will be done automatically if you include Technorati's RPC code in the list
of services you ping).

Creating Conversations on Blogs

Done the right way, commenting on other blogs can
bring a lot of relevant traffic to your own blog or web
site. Browse the Web, searching for blogs on your
niche. When you find a post that intrigues or interests you, and on which you think you can comment,
post a short note – and include a link back to your
blog.

Or you may prefer to use the 'Trackback' feature that

many blogs have. This allows you to post your comment on your blog, and let the other blog's owner know you've done it. Either way, you benefit: both from a link on the other targeted, related blog or website, and from traffic that may reach you from the other blog. If you don't have the time or interest to do this, you could outsource this task, too.

Social Bookmarking

Social bookmarking is all the rage today. And there's a service that makes it quick and convenient to handle multiple bookmarking sites easily.

Go to ONLYWIRE – http://www.OnlyWire.com. Once a free service, they now have a modestly-priced payment plan, though if you cannot afford it, there is an advertising-supported free one, as well. On the right side of the homepage, you will see a series of bookmarking services. Register for accounts with each. For convenience, you might want to use the same password for all, though it's up to you. Then, drag the bookmarklet to your web browser's status bar. This will make it easy to bookmark your blogs and sites at all these services.

When visitors to your blog find a post interesting, they too can bookmark your post to other social bookmarking sites, raising your blog's profile and attracting more visitors.

Social Networking

A very popular and attractive way to engage with your audience and draw many of them to your website or blog is to participate in discussions on online social networks. These are virtual communities where millions of people from all over the world meet, talk and share with others having similar interests.

Squidoo

A social networking service with great long-term potential is SQUIDOO (http://Squidoo.com). Based on the core concept that everyone is an expert at something, Squidoo provides users an easy website builder that can be tailored to any style, and will fit almost any subject or interest.

After signing up for a free account, explore the instruction manual to see how easy it is to set up your 'lens'. Notice how you can insert links to various sections of your own websites, blogs, and forum posts. There's even a blog module that pulls recent posts from your blog into your Squidoo lens automatically.

When you're ready to start building your first lens, work in links to these sections:

- Your blog

- Your website

- The specific forum sub-pages where your posts are published

Your social bookmark homepage - this is important, because it interlinks your various pages, building a bigger, more powerful authority network
And once you've set up your Squidoo lens, go ahead and post the URL to it in your blog, in your social

bookmark sites (del.icio.us, Jots and BlinkList) and even on forum posts!

Myspace

You can join millions of members who flock to one of the largest social networking sites on the Internet, MySpace.com. Open your own account at MySpace -- but make it specific to your niche site and business. Brand it with your business or website name. Include links to your site everywhere you can, without violating the terms of service.

MySpace even allows you to publish a blog. Post on your MySpace blog, sharing news and tidbits related to your niche, while sprinkling in links to your main blog. Participate in MySpace events. Send bulletins announcing events in your niche to your network of friends and contacts, and mention that further details are available on your blog.

Grow your network using various marketing techniques. Create a banner or button image including your URL to brand your business and/or product. That banner will show up on the pages of other friends whenever you are added on their network. You can even extend this further and create multiple profiles, targeting different keywords or sections of your site or business.

Facebook

Another huge social networking service is Facebook. By creating a profile on Facebook and making connections with people who are interested in

your niche, you can create another communication
channel between your product and your prospective
buyer. But, as with all other social networks, beware
of scooting down too many rabbit-holes and wasting
too much time on Facebook. Keep track of your time
involvement, measure the results it brings you in
your infopreneur business, and decide how active to
be on the network – or not!

Digg

Digg.com is another highly popular social networking service that can drive a flood of traffic your way.
Like most other publicity-oriented activities, you
need to approach this one with a good 'hook' that will
get your site a lot of popularity. Visitors to Digg vote
on any link; and the more popular ones get higher
visibility, which translates into more traffic.

Think of an 'angle' that works in your niche. Post a
catchy title on Digg, with a short description about
your niche site. You can tweak the results by asking
your blog readers to visit your listing on Digg and
vote on it. Do this even on the forums you frequent.
If enough readers visit and vote, you could get a flood
of new visitors to your site from Digg itself. And if
these new visitors like your site, they could keep
coming back again, and ultimately even become buyers.

Extreme Social Bookmarking

Bookmark your website on ONLYWIRE. There
are many other social bookmarks spanning niche
markets, and more coming online every day. Like

MySpace, there are sites like Orkut, Bebo, Magnolia and Friendster that have big networks of users. By setting up accounts on each of these services, you can get in front of these audiences, and attract a few of them to your site. OnlyWire makes this process simple and quick by submitting your link to all the social networking services for which you have registered.

Also, by linking together your accounts on these services with your MySpace, Squidoo, and other such sites, you'll be building a network of high-value links. This helps raise the profile of your website, and helps it rank higher on search engines, too.

Create An Authorative Resource

Imagine how it would be if you were to create a definitive document, a guide or resource or tip sheet that's 'best of breed' in your niche.

A resource like that would help hundreds, if not thousands, of people in your target market. Many other webmasters will point their readers and users to your resource, just because it gives them a chance to share enormous value with the readers.

It is a great idea to create your own authoritative resource. It could be a research report, a list of top 50 (or 100) tips, a definitive treatise on a specific subject, a huge compilation of the best resources: you get the idea. Your aim or goal should be to end up with the top information resource on the subject, bar none!

Then spread the word. Tell everyone you can about it. Make it easy for them to tell others. Let it 'go viral' and spread by word of mouth alone, reaching far beyond the limits of your own voice! You could speed up the process by inviting top experts in your niche to take a look. If one of them tells his or her big list about it, you could jumpstart your traffic and kick it into high gear!

And once on your site, visitors and prospective buyers will decide to stay and look around, even bookmark you and come back, based on the quality and extent of other content that you offer on your site. That is the reason why I obsessively insist on your continued blogging at least once every day!

Forum Marketing

Marketing and promoting your website on niche discussion forums is one of the best methods of attracting interested prospects to your website. In busy, interactive online communities, you must first take the time to understand the social dynamics before plunging in. But after you get a feel for how discussions progress, you should try to participate actively and promote your website subliminally.

Here's a technique that works well. Make a new post to your blog and try to include a reference to one of the newsworthy items on a forum discussion. This technique works best when it's something controversial, or provocative, or hot at the moment. Follow this simple sequence:

• Locate an interesting news story, article, or opinion/editorial relevant to your niche.

• Think about what you want to say.

• Type a short introduction or 'lead-in' to the material.

• Copy and paste an excerpt (short paragraph or snippet) from the article, news story, or website.

• Place a link to the rest of the story/article/website.

Then search on Google for forums, discussion groups, or bulletin boards on your niche topic. You can do this by searching on Google for 'Your Niche' + forums. Pick three of the busiest, most reputable, highest-ranking forums, where many people visit and post regularly. Register for an account on each one. Use your keywords in your user name, and craft your 'signature' to get some extra ranking benefit on search engines as well. Don't forget to include a link back to your website in the signature.

Now post a message that creates curiosity in a reader's mind. Use a headline like this:

• Have you read this news about ... ?

or

• Did you know ... ?

or

• What did you think about ... ?

In the body of your message, make a vague reference to the news story or article you blogged about. Do NOT give out all details, but hint about how important it could be to others in your niche. Then, sign off!

Here's what will happen. Either no one will be interested... which means you'll have to try again with a different 'angle'; or someone will reply with a comment or question. Very often, you'll get a post asking: 'Where can I read more about that?'

You reply by saying you just made a post to your blog, and that they can read all about it there. The link to your blog in your signature then acts as their road sign, bringing visitors to your blog. By going to the busiest, highest-ranked forums, you also make sure search engine spiders will 'find' your blog through your signature link.

Once you've established a presence in the top forums, keep it going by looking for another three to five forums after a week. Repeat the same system if it worked well before. Look at it this way: even if you don't get ANY interest or visits, the post with your signature file still counts as a link back to your site, giving you some benefit.

However, take care NEVER to violate the rules and spirit of the forum you are visiting. Abusing the privilege will get your post deleted, maybe get your account banned; and worse, it will brand you the wrong way with your target audience.

Write an Article

Creating informative, high-quality articles on the topic of your niche and submitting them to article directories and other resources where they will get maximum exposure is a great way to attract targeted visitors to your website.

Write a short article on any topic related to your niche. It should be between 450 and 600 words, include your main keyword around four to eight times, and maybe have your secondary keywords too. Try for around three to five paragraphs. Write short, simple sentences that are easily understood. Choose topics likely to interest readers in your niche. If you simply cannot write an article, you may consider outsourcing it to a writer. Expect to pay between $8 and $25 for a good-quality piece.

At the end, craft an attractive 'author resource box' mentioning the author's name, special skills, and something attractive about your website. Don't forget to include a link back to your site. You could even use keywords in this section to add relevance to the link. Make a mouth-watering offer that will draw readers back to your site – or even give them an email address so they can sign up to be on your mailing list).

When you are happy with your article, submit it only to the top article directories. These are good ones to start with:

Ezine Articles - http://EzineArticles.com

Go Articles - http://GoArticles.com

Article City - http://ArticleCity.com

Buzzle - http://Buzzle.com

Idea Marketers - http://IdeaMarketers.com

After a week, it's time to rinse and repeat the article
writing exercise. Same rules. Same process. Same
submission guidelines. But this time, you're going
wider, and trying to get your ad submitted to a large
number of article directories.

With well over 300 article directories out there, it's
kind of crazy to try and do it all by hand. You're better off using a software solution, or signing up with
a paid submission service, or hiring someone to do
it for you. Then submit your article far and wide: to
article directories, and even ezines and mailing lists
that accept outside contributions. Some paid submission services include:

iSnare - http://iSnare.com

Article Marketers - http://ArticleMarketers.com

Phantom Writers - http://ThePhantomWriters.com

There are also many software programs to help you
do this submission semi-automatically. By doing this
every week, over and over, you will create another
major traffic stream to your site.

CONTENT REPOSITORIES AND HIGH TRAFFIC SITES

Ehow

Ehow.com is an interesting site, with a high page
rank and a lot of traffic. It is a 'how to' style resource

where you can contribute a short 'how to' article on your niche. Spend some time looking around. Brainstorm ideas for creating a 'how to' for your niche. See if someone else has written one. If not, compose and post it, with a link back to your site and blog.

Yahoo Answers

Ever wonder how answering questions someone asks online can boost your site's traffic? Yahoo Answers and Google Answers are services where people can ask questions and have experts answer them. Look for questions related to your niche, and answer them. You might have to do some research to find the answer, but that's time well worth spending. The best answers will be featured prominently, giving your links more visibility, and getting your website more traffic.

Yahoo Groups

Yahoo Groups (and Google Groups) are high-page-rank sites, which get spidered very regularly by search engines. A not-very-well-known 'trick' to get traffic and quickly have search engines rank your new website is to set up your own Yahoo Groups account and tie it in with your niche site.

An added advantage is that you can link your list-building to the Yahoo mailing server, allowing you to mail your ezine through their service. Remember, you are doing this primarily to get exposure, to obtain links back to your page, and to drive some traffic. The discussion and community are nice 'extras'.

Craig's List

Craig's List - http://CraigsList.org - is one of the biggest classified ad services on the Net. It's a great way to drive targeted traffic to your site.

Caution: Do NOT abuse it. The site is heavily moderated, and you risk losing your account and future posting privileges if you violate the terms and conditions. Be very careful. Read the guidelines and instructions for posting classified ads before you begin.

Again, you have two goals. The first is to get your site spidered by search engine scripts (called 'robots') which crawl Craig's List many times every day. The second is to get human visitors who are interested in your topic to visit your site.

In most cases, you can only post your ad to the 'Small Business Ads' section. Use text in your ad description that includes your keywords, so that you will get benefits of inbound linking. Your ad will be removed after seven days, but you can repost it again later. You may NOT post the same ad multiple times across the service.

Other Techniques

Apart from the techniques detailed above, I'll mention a random selection of traffic-driving techniques you may want to try out.

1 Gather.com. This is a site like Squidoo; it is growing fast, and has potential to bring some more visitors to your main site.

2.Wikipedia.com. This is a collaborative content
resource that grows by contributors adding to and
expanding on the material on the site. By writing
content for Wikipedia about your niche, you could
enhance your visibility.

3 Collaborative wikis. There are other 'wikis' like
Wikipedia on various niches. You could obtain links
from these in the same way as with Wikipedia, by
writing niche-specific content.

Affiliate Marketing

This may not be relevant if you do not sell a product
or service, or have no interest in working with affiliates and joint venture partners. But it is one of
the most powerful traffic-driving approaches; and,
though it will take some time and effort to put in
place, you don't spend any money upfront. For that
reason, this is a very attractive system for beginners
to follow.

To sign up affiliates, you need a software solution
(either a standalone affiliate management system or
one that comes bundled with your web hosting account). Of course, if you are on a shoestring budget,
you can begin without one, running your affiliate
program on a service like Clickbank (http://Click-
bank.com) which handles all affiliate management
issues.

Find the top 'players' in your niche. Write, call, or
meet them. Explain your online business to them.
Focus on how you think you can help them and their
clients, readers, subscribers. Make your offer as at-

tractive as possible, making it easier for them to say
'Yes' than 'No'.

Remember, while this initial offer may not be imme-
diately profitable to you, you are building assets that
will stand with you, supporting your infopreneur
business for years. You will quickly acquire a list of
customers, and can sell them many more things in
the future. You will also develop a group of partners
who will be glad to work with you later, if you make
this first experience pleasant and profitable. Stay focused on the long term goal, and your JV experience
will be pleasurable and fun.

First, try to contact at least three partners who
agree to help you promote. Keep making contacts
daily, until you have a core group of at least ten partners, with a combined audience of 50,000 prospects
or more. Sound impossible? It's easy: many top players have lists far bigger than this!

Search on Google for the top resources. Look on
forums for the senior, experienced marketers. Study
affiliate sites to identify top super-affiliates. Then
contact them to help drive traffic to your site and sell
your products and services to their lists. If you make
it worth their time and effort, some of those you approach for a deal will agree to do business with you.

Press Releases

Press releases are a great, free way to gain visibility
for your infopreneur business and attract a large
audience interested in your niche.

Try and look for something newsworthy in your business, and draft a press release around it. The aim of your release is to get reporters interested in doing a follow up story; so you need a 'hook' and an 'angle'. You can learn about writing press releases from excellent online resources like B.L.Ochman's www. WhatsNextBlog.com and Paul Hartunian's site www. PaulHartunian.com.

When you're done, distribute your press release to sites like PR Web (http://PRweb.com), which not only give you publicity, but also a high-value inbound link to your website. You did include your URL, didn't you?

With the right approach – and some luck – your press release could result in free advertising for you and your business. Better still, it might even ripple and spread further, landing you on prime-time TV or the front page of a national newspaper!

Google Adwords

Were you expecting this to be the cornerstone of the traffic driving blueprint?
Most courses about traffic focus on Google Adwords and other pay-per-click (PPC) services as the primary method, because PPC is quick, targeted, and guaranteed.

It is also expensive.

That's why I don't like to use PPC until the other parts of the process have been tested and tweaked. You should have gotten enough visitors to your site to test out your mechanisms. Does your sales letter convert prospects into buyers? Does your opt-in form

attract enough subscribers to join your newsletter?
Does your payment processor work? Are other things
in order?

Only after you've tested and tweaked these should
you invest cash into driving more traffic to your site.
At this stage, Adwords is the quickest, most effective method. Set up your Google Adwords account.
Learn about running PPC campaigns. There are
many excellent courses on the subject of PPC advertising. Run your ads only after picking your best
keywords for the campaign. Start small. Test and
track everything. Cut your losses and let your win-
ners ride.

By carefully optimizing the process, one change at
a time, you will soon have a profitable, sustainable
Adwords campaign that earns you more income than
you spend on advertising. Remember what my teacher, Jay Abraham, is fond of saying: "The only risk you
ever have to take in business is an inexpensive test".
So carry out your tests, and analyze your results.

Expand Your PPC Adverticing

Once you have a fair idea if your Google Adwords
campaign is profitable, you can decide whether or
not to expand it. If it is, then roll it out on a bigger
scale. Add new keywords. Raise your daily budget.
Experiment with other variables.

And if it is not profitable, look into the reasons why –
and fix them.

Another thing to do if you have a 'winning formula' is
to replicate it across other PPC services like Yahoo!

Search Marketing and MSN's AdCenter PPC program. There are many more such services. You can find a complete list at PayPerClickSearchEngines. com.

Always keep a close watch on your numbers. Make sure you are profitable; or pause the campaign until you can fix what's broken. Failure to do this one thing has capsized many fledgling businesses, putting them deep into debt and destroying them.

Ezine And Email ADs

Again, this method involves expense, and is not guaranteed. Yes, you might get a great response. On the other hand, you might not get any response at all. A lot depends upon how well targeted your offer is to the audience who reads the ezine or email in which you advertise. So spend some time picking the best ezines for your advertisements.

Charlie Page's 'Directory of Ezines' - http://DirectoryofEzines.com - has a comprehensive listing of email newsletters that accept advertisements. Ezine Articles has a good resource collection, too. You might even test out email solo advertising using paid ads, or services like Opportunity.com, ListDotCom. com, and Solo-Ads.com for your testing. As with PPC advertising, the trick to staying profitable is to test small, track carefully, and tweak frequently, until you have a winner.

Mail Your In-House List

You're getting some traffic. And some of your visitors will opt-in to join your email list (you did put up a form on all parts of your site and blog, didn't you?) The best way to get a quick burst of traffic to your website is to send out a short email promotion to your in-house list. This is the best kind of traffic: targeted, trusting, ready to buy or take action.

Working with mailing lists, building trusting relationships, and marketing to subscribers are skills that take time and experience to acquire and master. But at the very least, sending your subscribers a short note to invite them back to your blog, where you post content valuable to them, is a good use of your mailing list. In time, this alone could be very profitable.

Publish An Email Newsletter

This is optional, but effective. Take the concept of mailing your in-house list a step further by publishing an email newsletter (or ezine). Instead of just inviting them back to your blog, you could send them valuable content on a periodic schedule, by email. What content? Articles, tips, links, news tidbits, industry development, special offers, resources: any and all of these can be content for your ezine.

Publish your ezine on a weekly basis. Include one of your weekly articles in it, with summaries of your blog posts, and useful links you find on forums you visit. Then, invite readers back to your site, and even pre-sell them on your products and services – all via email.

Linking Strategies

You are now at the point where you need to build more links back to your site. It is growing steadily, with content on your blog and articles. It is getting more visitors from the promotion you've done. Now, you need more links.

There are two ways to get them:

1. Create a reciprocal linking directory on your site where related webmasters can come to exchange links with your site. Many scripts are available to automate the process and make it run hands-free. You could install a script like 'Reciprocal Manager' on your website. Services like LinkMetro.com bring together webmasters seeking link swaps, and streamline the actual process of exchanging links.

2. Work on a one-way inbound link campaign. This is harder, but more valuable. You (or someone you train) can contact owners of websites in your niche which are highly ranked and contain great content. Request a link back to your content-rich website from theirs. It may take some going back and forth, even getting on the phone or writing a letter; but if it works, this could boost your site's ranking on search engines higher than most other marketing tasks you will perform.

When setting up one-way links, try to get the other webmaster to include your choice of keyword as the anchor text of your inbound link, so you get more value from the link. Strive for a target of five high-quality links per week, and within a year, you could have around 250 links. That will go a long way toward making your site an AUTHORITY site in your niche.

Compile a Free Ebook Or Report

By the time you have written three or four articles, some blog posts, and answered a few questions on Yahoo Answers, you have enough original content on hand to compile into a short ebook or report. If you do it, this will give you another traffic-driving vehicle.

Create a PDF document with your niche content. Sprinkle it with links pointing back to your website. Then give it away to everyone. List it on all free ebook directories you can find. Offer redistribution rights to others in your niche, so they can spread it around. You might even put a price tag on it to heighten the perceived value. If the quality of your content is high, the ebook could get distributed and passed along virally, driving even more traffic back to your site.

This is by no means a comprehensive marketing guide. It is meant to be a quick-start guide that can help drive some targeted traffic to your new website within 30 days. To learn how to take it further, and to tie in other offline marketing strategies to your promotion, take a look at the Internet Infopreneur System course at http://www.InternetInfopreneur.com.

Ramp It Up!
Build Your Infopreneuring into an Information Empire

With the hardest part of the process behind you, it's time to set things up to profit continuously, automatically, for many years to come. It is neither difficult nor effort- intensive; but it does need these simple, calculated tweaks to maximize your long-term profitability.

Many years ago, when I was a kid, I heard this story about a wise old sage who lived in the foothills of the majestic Himalayas. One day, to teach his disciples a valuable lesson, he picked the five smartest boys.

He blindfolded them tightly so they could see nothing. Then he led them into the forest. He took them to an elephant; allowed them to feel different parts of the animal; then asked them to describe what they 'saw'.

The first boy felt the animal's leg and said it was like a tree-trunk. The second held the elephant's tail, and said it felt like a rope. The third disciple, holding the trunk, thought it was like a thick snake. The fourth, touching the pointy tusk, feared it was a spear, while the last claimed the large flapping ears reminded him of a palm leaf.

When the blindfolds were removed, and each one saw the elephant they had been touching, their amazed faces turned red in embarrassment!

So, what's this got to do with being an infopreneur?

Just this: regardless of our level of experience and expertise, most of us infopreneurs are like the blindfolded boys. We see different, incomplete parts of the picture, and think we have 'tamed the beast', cracked the code, and mastered the field!

Until the veil parts, and you see the 'next level'.

Well, this section is about to rip off your blindfold – and reveal in stark detail the many dimensions of being an Internet infopreneur! You'll read about the various approaches to understanding and mastering these dimensions, and the vital importance of not getting stuck at your present level, but constantly striving for growth and progress.

This is information I wish I had received and read while getting started a decade ago. If only it had been available to me then, things might have taken a different course entirely.

With zero business or marketing knowledge at the time, I stumbled my way into these 'infopreneur secrets', one at a time, over years – often paying a heavy price for the wisdom gained.

I hope it will help you formulate your own strategy and action plan intelligently and with all relevant information.

The Three Drivers of Online Business

The theme of this section is the Three 'P's:

PHILOSOPHY, PURPOSE and PROCESS.

PHILOSOPHY is about mindset. And there are as

many different ones as there are business owners.

Some flit and fleet from one experiment to another, hopping around in a constant, never-ending quest for that elusive 'big hit'. The cost of starting a business in the real world keeps this number small. But in the virtual environment of the Internet, where the cost of entry is much lower, this is a malaise that affects 95% or more of home businesses.

A few 'lucky' folks outgrow this phase of constant change. After some casual flings, they finally hit upon a 'winner' and settle down to milk their cash-cow. But no more than three out of every hundred home business owners do this well. More often, they get caught up in the 'wanderlust' syndrome and stray off the narrow path again and again.

And then you have the 'cherry picker'. This savvy business-person experiments with different approaches, and is smart enough to find the elements of each that work well. Armed with enough such information, this infopreneur is now in the advantageous position of owning industry 'best practices'. These can be implemented in a consistent fashion to guarantee reasonable success at anything.

Rare indeed is the small group of strategic business owners who go about their task with a single-minded devotion backed by rich experience and/or real knowledge. These experts choose wisely, stick with their choice, and work on steadily growing and improving it. Of course, to do this well, you must make sure the choice you make in the first place is the right one.

The big question, then, becomes: "Why not become strategic yourself?"

The short answer: "Because it is NOT easy"

The 'mind mapping' underlying this comes, I suspect, a bit more naturally to someone who has owned and operated a successful offline business.

It requires a certain level of expert knowledge (or real life experience, often earned after a series of smaller mistakes). It makes mandatory a considerable amount of research and investigation to find that perfect 'niche' in the marketplace. It involves focused effort, and often a modest financial investment to build the business in a structured, scalable fashion.

And once that's done, it takes some ongoing involvement to position it for quick, even explosive growth. It needs to be based on 'automated' systems that make it possible for the owner to step away from the business, and yet have it hum along smoothly.

PURPOSE is all about your 'reason why'. It is the fuel that drives the engine of all your other business activities. It is the axle around which your business wheel revolves. It is your consuming, inspiring, motivating 'Why' – whatever that might be.

For many home business owners, it is based around either 'escape from pain' (getting out of the 9-to-5 grind, or avoiding an intolerable boor who happens to be your boss) or a 'search for gain' (an extra bit of income, small comforts, a better lifestyle with perks).

A few dream bigger. They aim to achieve wealth through building a roaring business... right from the beginning. The approach they take to their online business is more aggressive, proactive, and intensive.

Time, money and effort are viewed as investments rather than expenses. Acquiring knowledge and tapping into others' expertise are considered business-building essentials rather than frivolous luxuries.

Within this group is a sub-group of business owners who play the 'build, grow and sell' game, and do it well. The essential difference in attitude between these people and the rest is the emphasis placed on 'systems'.

These business owners meticulously strive to keep their own personality out of the way of their business functions, so that they do NOT become an irreplaceable part of the system. In turn, this makes the business easier to flip and sell to new owners, often at huge profits.

Again, the difference lies in your underlying strategy – or lack of it.

Does your infopreneur business have a formal plan? Has your growth been structured, organized, and consistent? Is your business scalable, replicable, and saleable?

Chances are high that the answers to all these questions are a resounding "NO". Don't let that get you down: you're in the company of the vast majority of Internet business owners and online marketers. The good news is, now you know about it, there's time to make a change!

<u>PROCESS</u> is the step-by-step approach to making that change. It is the deep understanding of the three online business models we discussed earlier. It is identifying your strengths and competitive advantages, and integrating them into the 'best fit' model. And it is unique to YOU.

Look, no one model is 'better' or 'perfect'. Each one has success stories. And each model has followers who failed miserably, trying to get it to work for them.

The reasons for that are diverse. You have a unique personality. Your risk tolerance is different from that of others. You have skills, training, experience that sets you apart from every other business owner in the world. Your resources – time, money, assistants – are not the same as those available to other business owners. Your willingness to experiment, your ability to make swift, effective changes and adaptations, your 'teachability': all define how well, or how poorly, you will do in going after one of the three models.

A quick example might help clarify this. Let's say you feel uncomfortable in a selling situation. You hate trying to convince a prospect to buy something from you. If you try out the 'direct selling' model, you'll very likely fail at it; or at least, you won't succeed as easily as you would at one of the others.

On the other hand, a person who is passionate about selling will out-perform you – even with a poorer product, a less-impressive website, a smaller budget. And that's because she will be playing to her strengths.

So, in a nutshell, that's the 'wisdom' that's taken me almost a decade of learning to gain. This is relatively scarce information that I haven't seen discussed so explicitly anywhere else – even though I've spent several thousand dollars on information products, courses, seminars, ebooks, reports, and other learning material over the years!

What's a Good Approach to Picking Your Model?

Judging by the way I've seen most beginners seek their way through the confusion on their way to set up an infopreneur business on the Internet, the 'conventional' approach is to start by researching a market and finding a need.

Once the need has been identified, the infopreneur tries to create a solution, build a sales process, generate leads for the product or service, and convert a sufficient number of leads into buyers or customers. Then the twin growth 'strategies' of getting more customers and selling them more stuff kick in, growing the business sky-high.

Incidentally, this is also the way I got started years ago. You've probably heard, read, or seen many people advocate this approach. And they are not wrong. It's just that they leave out some critical components. They probably rationalize that too much discordant information served up at the begin-

ning will scare away too many eager starters from
ever entering the race.

But personally, I think that's a mistake. Why paint
building an infopreneur business on the Internet as
a simple thing even a child can do easily, when the
reality is quite different? No, it's not rocket science.
Still, setting up a home business online is a definite,
structured, sometimes difficult process.

It most certainly is not an impulsive, spur-of-the-
moment thing to conceive, plan, build, and grow a
business – even an Internet business – to success!
But here's a question that one of my mentors asked,
and which has guided my actions in my own infopreneur business since then:

> "Why run your online activities as a hobby when,
> with a little planning, directed effort, and strate-
> gic implementation, you can run your hobby as a
> real business – and earn many times more from it,
> while working less and having more fun?"

When I first heard these words, I missed their real
impact. Gradually, the power in this statement has
opened my eyes – and fattened my wallet! So, let me
ask the critical question all over again:

What's the Best Approach to Planning Your On-
line Infopreneuring Business?

I hate to sound like an M.B.A. (I'm not one, by the
way!), but the best method would be to make a formal
assessment of your strengths and weaknesses, and
thus identify your suitability to a particular approach.

Success is primarily a mindset. Once you believe
you can succeed, you certainly will. And it's easier
to believe when your infopreneur business is built
around your strengths, than when you set sail in un-
charted waters, feeling your way through, not knowing exactly what you're doing.

Finding a niche is important. Finding one that's
aligned to your strengths is critical. Identifying
a market's need is essential. Finding one you can
solve based upon your own (or your team's) strengths
is vital.

Begin With Your End in Mind

I've gone on a while, but still haven't even touched
upon the nitty-gritty of business-building. There's a
reason for that.

Unless you have your PHILOSOPHY and PURPOSE
perfected, your PROCESS is not going to help you
much. It is worth spending time, effort, even money,
to identify these critical drivers of your long-term
business success – before you even start doing anything like niche research or market surveys.

After all, as one wise man said, "If you don't know
where you're going, how will you know when you get
there?"

Assuming you have defined, clearly and in explicit
detail, why you are getting into building an online
infopreneur business, and what you expect to do
with it once you're up and running: there's still a lot
of groundwork to be done.

It is challenging. It is exhausting. It is fun.

So don't let yourself be frightened away by the thought of how forbidding, scary, and huge the task seems. I'm going to break it down for you into smaller, bite-sized chunks so you can pick apart the business-building elements and tackle them one at a time, all the while knowing that what you are working on will ultimately fit together seamlessly into an integrated whole that pulls everything together.

The Four-Dimensional Picture of Your Online Business

It's strange how, when you go deeper into the intricacies of each component of business building, you discover the parts fit together into a picture that's effective and elegantly simple in its breadth and scope.

Though hard to explain, I've tried to paint a picture of it for you – in FOUR dimensions!

FIRST Dimension: Creating your business processes
SECOND Dimension: Automating your processes
THIRD Dimension: Outsourcing your processes
FOURTH Dimension: Optimizing your processes

Stage by stage, this four-dimensional approach will allow you to build your infopreneur business, save yourself time and effort in managing it, and get it growing by leaps and bounds. Before you know it, you'll have the choice of either keeping it and enjoying the profits for a long time, or selling it off for a windfall.

The FIRST Dimension

The journey of a thousand miles begins with a single step.

Your first one is to plan and create the different steps – 'processes' – that make up your Internet infopreneur business. No matter whether you picked the direct selling model or the content publishing model, they have some things in common that you must do in the correct sequence.

We have already gone through some of them in greater detail in earlier chapters, but I'm going to leave you with this brief summary of what it's all about.

1. Niche Research

Look for a problem out there in the marketplace that you can help solve. See what bothers people, and think about a solution you can offer them.Another approach is to see what's 'hot' – wildly-popular trends that many thousands are following – and come up with an offer you can extend to them.

The critical questions to ask yourself during your niche research are these:

• Is the niche big enough?
• Is the niche profitable enough?
• Is the niche easily targeted and reached
• Is the niche scalable?

In other words, are there enough people looking for

the solution you plan to offer? Do they have money, and are they willing to spend it on your   solution? Where do your prospects gather, how do they interact, and what ways can you get your marketing message in front of them? And if you become a big hit, is there any way you can then grow your business further within the niche, or extend it out to new sub-niches, and do it easily and economically?

2. Mindset and Belief Systems

Once you've located a niche to pursue, you need to sit back and ask yourself an important question:

"Can I do it?"

The answer to this question determines, in large part, your success or failure.

If you enter into the hottest, most competitive niche, but believe firmly in your mind that you cannot win because you are going up against smart, deep-pocketed marketers, you'll very likely fail.

On the other hand, if you view it as a challenge, and set out with optimism, ready to try to break into the system, knowing you will win at any cost,   your chances of massive success just multiplied!

3. Planning and Strategy

You need a business plan. It should be detailed, elaborate, and practical.

Assess your strengths and weaknesses, and those of your competition. Include detailed market analysis.

Make a list of opportunities and your plans to take advantage of them. Spell out targets and goals. Estimate costs and investments. Chalk out deadlines and time frames.

Create detailed process charts for every aspect of your infopreneur business. Trace each step from beginning to end, explaining how things will work, and defining who takes responsibility for each step.

Prepare for growth. If your business will be growing steadily, outline the plan for it. How will it happen? On what time schedule? Which areas will get priority?

Assemble your team. Study your plan to see which skills you already have in-house, and which ones you need to recruit or hire. Share your plan with your team, so you're all on the same page.

4. Tools and Resources

Like any other real-world business, your Internet business too requires certain essential elements. You'll use tools like statistics analysis programs, scripts to run split tests and track ads, autoresponder email services to follow up with prospects, web hosting services to store your files, and many more.

One crucial element for which many businesses fail to budget is education. A commitment to ongoing learning is your biggest competitive advantage. On the Internet, technology shifts so rapidly it will make your head spin. Keeping up with new trends is not an option – it's a necessity.

Another important, yet frequently ignored, resource is finding and keeping skilled people to handle specialized tasks. Experts at copywriting, system administration, and graphic editing are worth their weight in gold. If you find good helpers, make sure you do your best to keep them happy, so that they won't run away and work with your competition!

5. Building Your Web Presence

This is the point at which most business building courses begin – and end! Yet, as you've seen, there is a lot to be done BEFORE this stage, and a lot more to be done after.

You'll create (or get licensing rights) to an information product or service, build a website for your business, construct a sales process (including writing a great sales letter), set up a payment processing system to handle online transactions securely, place name/address capture forms on your site, organize a method to follow up with prospective buyers, and more.

At a later stage, you'll incorporate affiliate marketing systems and joint venture arrangements for further growth.

6. Testing and Tweaking

Once you've got your basic setup ready, it's time to start driving visitors to your website sales letter (or sending out the letters to prospects by mail) and seeing how the process performs. Testing is hard work – and the most important thing you'll do.

Everything else being equal, testing is the single activity that will give you the highest return on your investment by helping you improve conversion and boosting profits.

Any online business is a work in progress. There is absolutely no limit to which you can enhance and improve your business, and testing each element is the right way to go about it.

7. Relationship Building

After the backbone of your online business is in place, you'll focus on the more powerful things like relationship building with your clients and visitors, to ensure future growth and viability.

List-building is a critical business skill. Publishing an email newsletter (or ezine) is one way to keep in touch with your prospects. So is publishing a blog (or weblog) and distributing an RSS feed. Discussion forums, bulletin boards, and email interactive lists also help foster a sense of community and keep visitors coming back to your website.

Each of these is a specialized field in itself. By focusing on one of these at a time, creating a process for each, and testing it until you are satisfied with the results, you will ensure steady growth for your infopreneur business. Then, by applying strategy based on the second and third dimension, you will further streamline them and hone their efficiency.

8. Traffic Generation

After everything in your business process has been

tested and perfected, your next business-growth driver is increased traffic. Get more visitors to your website. Mail your sales letters to more prospects. Advertise more aggressively. Involve your visitors and customers in the activity, by putting in place referral systems, launching your own affiliate program, and getting delighted customers to help with growing your business.

All else being the same, a site that gets 10,000 visitors will naturally out-perform the one with 1,000 visitors. So, on the Web, more traffic is a good thing (as long as the traffic is targeted to your business).

Traffic-generation systems could be technology-driven (like blogs and RSS (feeds), content-driven (like article submissions and syndication), money-driven (like pay-per-click traffic from search engines or paid targeted traffic), or people-driven (from affiliates and link partners).

As I mentioned earlier, please try to look beyond the specific solutions I'm listing here, to see the underlying principle. Build your infopreneur business, one element after the other. Test each stage and make changes to improve results. Drive a flood of targeted traffic to the site. Your business can't help growing.

The SECOND Dimension

While the action steps outlined in the first part are essential, they are also the hardest for a new business owner to implement. Most of the steps are new, technical, and require time and money to set up. However, every business owner needs to take them.

Sadly, though, at this point most beginners ease off and begin to relax. This is a mistake, because the strategies in the second and third stages take less time and effort to implement. Paradoxically, they can save you a lot more time, allowing you to focus on other business-building activities!

Look at business process automation, for instance. I'll use the example of a typical direct-selling-model business. The product is an ebook. Here's how the sales process would look:

- Prospect arrives at website
- Reads sales letter
- Decides either to buy or to leave (at which point, the prospect is invited to sign up to receive a free ezine)
- Clicks on the order button and makes a payment
- Receives instructions to download the ebook.

By setting up this process intelligently, the business owner can have it all run entirely hands-free. The website could sell literally a thousand copies of the ebook every day, while the business owner is on vacation!

It is, however, possible to take the automation a notch higher. Let's say one in a hundred buyers has a technical problem with the ebook download. This means that if you make 1,000 sales, you'll get ten requests for technical assistance. How to tackle it?

One solution is to create a section on your website for 'Frequently Asked Questions'. Give all buyers a link to it, so they can find the answers. Another solution is to have download details emailed again to buyers through an email autoresponder. A third solution is to have a copy of the ebook itself emailed to buyers as an attachment. A fourth is to hire a customer service and support assistant, and set this person up with a help desk system that logs complaints, and allows them to resolve problems – while giving you, the business owner, control over the overall process.

Any of these solutions (and there are more) will eliminate the ten customer service requests due to ebook download problems, thus saving the business owner precious time.

The good news is, with careful planning and some creative thinking, many processes in an infopreneur business can be similarly automated. Some solutions require custom programming skills. Others require analytical thinking about each step in the process. There may be a cost involved in implementing the solution. Almost always, it is well worth the investment; because over the long term, these simple changes will save you hours of time and tons of aggravation, while helping build client loyalty.

The THIRD Dimension

Even with the best intentions, you cannot automate EVERYTHING in your business. There will still be some 'human touch' points that will require personal involvement by your team (though with a well-planned, aggressively-imposed approach, these will be very few).

Let's take the content publishing model for this example.

In this model, practically everything can be automated, right from the content creation to posting on the
website, updating, framing with contextual advertising, adding fresh content, and more.

However, there are some steps that still need human
intervention: things like niche keyword research, for
example, or selecting a website template to use.

As a third-dimension business owner, you have a
choice. You can keep these few tasks to yourself, and
have them done in-house by your own team; or you
can transcend even these limitations by outsourcing
these processes.

Doing this effectively involves a little more planning
and the creation of systems. Let's use the keyword
research example again. To outsource this, your
business will need to create a set of detailed guidelines for a helper to follow while picking keywords.

The upside is that by doing it once and documenting
your process, you now free yourself of the need to do
it repeatedly. And by having the step outsourced,
you now give yourself extra time and energy to work
on another element of your business — or even do
something else entirely.

Let me emphasize this point again: the limits of
what (and how much) you can outsource are really
up to your imagination. Some businesses with high
earnings are run by a handful of in-house employees,
with all other tasks being outsourced to freelancers.

It all boils down to your PHILOSOPHY and PUR-
POSE. Do you now see how vital those elements are

to the way your entire business process operates?
When you start with the end in mind, decisions
about specific issues become easier, clearer, and consistent with other decisions.

And everything in your business starts working
according to your overarching strategic objectives,
rather than being governed by day-to-day, 'whim and
fancy' tactical thinking.

The FOURTH Dimension

Effective implementation of the steps discussed
above will result in a profitable, efficient, fully-automated online business that chugs along regardless of
where you are, or what you are doing.

It's this kind of business that makes the owner
money "in your sleep"!

No, it's not a pipe-dream. It could become your
dream too, if you are willing to buckle down and
take whatever action is necessary to make it happen. Once you've set all this up, you may be tempted
to think there's little left to do. You'd be wrong – but
pleasantly so. There's still one more tweak you can
apply to your web-based home business that will
help harvest hidden windfall profits inside it. It's a
set of 'tricks' called 'Business Optimization'.

Let me share with you a personal experience of using one such technique. This is a real case study. It
may not be earth-shaking news - but it's pretty neat.
In late 2004, I launched a product called the 'Niche
Starter Kit'. The regular kit cost $19.95. In the sales
process, I implemented an optimization strategy. In

three months, we made 142 sales in total. And 65 of these buyers spent 62% MORE than they would have otherwise – making us $4,591 instead of $2,832

Would you believe it if I told you that a simple change in a headline could boost your ad responsiveness by nine times or more? Would you believe that you could get nearly 50% more sales from selling the same product to the same list if you utilize another power principle? Yet that's really what's possible if you apply a business-optimization strategy to your process.

Here's what makes this most attractive: it is much easier to put into action than any of the initial steps that are essential to a business!

That's right. Over 90% of business owners put in all the hard work to get a barely- functional business process in place – but then hesitate to work just a little bit harder to institute a set of optimization steps that could literally TRIPLE profits!

There are eight major levers, and many more minor ones, that when pulled can give your business a profit jolt. Harnessing their power is one of the biggest aspects of leverage in your online business. You'll find a brief overview of them at http://www.5xProfits. com.

Rolex Watches and Information Marketing

Many years ago, there was an ad for a Rolex. In
great detail, the ad explained what went on beneath
the dial. It included beautiful pictures showing
dozens of interlocking ratchets, with wheels within
wheels. Each tiny, perfectly hand-crafted element
was responsible for a critical function.

They all integrated perfectly, worked in synchronic-
ity, and coordinated wonderfully.

Information product marketing – being an infopreneur – is somewhat like that.

There are dozens of components, and each is intri-
cately interlinked with the other. The combination
works cohesively to power an online business and
fire up profits.

It is important to know, understand, and master
each individual component. But the way most
currently-available courses, ebooks and programs
present them, it is easy for a student to think that
each one is a stand-alone 'system' that works inde-
pendently of the others; and that mastering one is a
guarantee of lifelong profitability!

Nothing could be further from the truth.

Certainly one (or a few) techniques may work better
or worse than others for you. But if you risk your
business by focusing on any one of them to the exclu-
sion of others, you are setting yourself up for failure
– and taking a huge risk. Integrating together all
the disparate elements we have discussed will help

you build a sustainable infopreneur business, one designed to survive and thrive under any circumstance.
And that's how you will 'Think, Write and RETIRE!'

But just as with the Rolex, each component has finer
details and nuances which are hard to explain in
detail in an overview of this kind. That's why I am
supplementing it with a more detailed, step by step,
comprehensive course about building an information
marketing business on the Internet.

In it you will discover many more helpful resources,
learn the nitty-gritty details that go into creating
every part of the process, and have anytime access
to a reference book that will guide you from the start
to building your first information product, making
sales, and then leveraging that success into a complete infopreneur business. This course is called
"The Internet Infopreneur SYSTEM". You can find
more details from the website at http://www.Inter-
netInfopreneur.com.

Make This Your New Beginning!

I hope you've found this overview of building an online information business helpful.

With what you have learned in 'Think, Write & Retire' you can go out and build the information business empire of your dreams. All it takes is focus, persistence and action.

Where I Started - And You Can Too

Nearly 15 years ago, I built my first website. Soon after, I created my first infoproduct. It was about something I knew well, was an expert, where not many others could compete.

Since then, that one information product - a short special report - has sold 348 copies at a price of $39.95... literally on auto-pilot (all I do today is renew the domain name and pay for web hosting - once in a year!).

That's over $1,000 every year, for 11 years, from just one product - with no work after the initial set up.

Over the years, I have created and sold another 64 different kinds of information products (priced from $7 to $997) - and many more I did not even create myself! By packaging and presenting the same information in different formats, I have created multiple unique income streams to monetize the material and boost profits.

In all, this infopreneuring empire has sold over quarter million dollars worth of products - entirely over the Internet!

The amazing part is that right now, you too have some valuable information locked up in your own brain... that people - many people - will gladly pay you to share with them.

You Too Have AT LEAST One Profitable Info-Product Inside You

Let Me Help You Find It!

This short book has barely scratched the surface of what it takes to build and nurture a successful online infopreneur business. For some readers, this is all that's needed. They can manage the rest.

Still, each of the individual sections we looked at in this book contains many more, and finer, details to study, apply, and optimize. And the one thing experience has taught me is that different people have different needs. Some can take a bare-bones outline, flesh it out and adapt it to their skills and resources. Others will be baffled by the same outline, and wish for more details, guidance and support.

If I stopped here and left you hanging, it would be fair neither to you, nor to the many business coaches and mentors who taught me, shared their wisdom and knowledge selflessly, and in many ways are responsible for my online success.

That is why I decided to do something about it for

readers of this book like you who are interested in getting more detailed information on building, growing, and optimizing your Internet Infopreneur home business.

I started looking at the problem, and came up with this solution.

• What if I could put together a comprehensive course covering every single aspect of information product creation and marketing?

• What if I outlined the very same steps and process smart infopreneurs go through when planning and launching a product?

• What if I give beginners all the tools needed to tap into the powerful and valuable material lying idle in their head?

• What if I revealed my most lucrative trade secrets so anyone can tap into an eager, hungry, ready-to-buy market?

• What if they can use this training to create an info-product empire that grows and swells into a steady business, bringing in profits automatically for years?

Wouldn't that be 'interesting' to budding infopreneurs like you who hope to earn money working online?

That's the reason I offer a supplemental program called "The Internet Infopreneur System" at http:// InternetInfopreneur.com

In this program, you will receive a complete, step by step blueprint to build a massively profitable infopreneur business within one year... and take the first step on your exciting journey to becoming an Internet infopreneur today.

If you have a sincere work ethic, can follow instructions, and are serious about learning how to create information products and profit from them in multiple ways including selling them over the Internet, and are looking for in-depth guidance, instruction and support, you will find this program useful.

In a nutshell, here is the biggest advantage you will gain from taking this course after reading this book...

It will be easy, quick and fun to do all that you have just learned. The number of times you fail will be less. Your chances will be brighter of sticking with it and seeing it through, instead of throwing up your hands in frustration and giving up.

And if this sounds overwhelming and huge, take a deep breath and relax. We're about to take aim at all the confusion and 'darkness' out there, shine a bright torch into the gloom and light up your trail to infopreneur success.

Learn At Your Own Pace
Right From Home

In this course, I will be guiding you through a sequential process with elaborate, specific and detailed tutorials.

• I'll show you how to tap into your hidden assets to come up with 'killer' information products and content resources.

• I'll teach you how to find eager audiences of prospective buyers and find out what they want you to give them.

• I'll walk you through creating your infoproduct, selling it, and then repeating the process or setting it on auto-pilot to grow automatically.

• I'll reveal multiple alternative ways you can leverage this specialized information to create different income streams flowing into your business.

Six months from now, you too will be one of my success stories - delighted with your achievements and excited about your potential.

This program is...

Your Key To Quickly Build Strong, Sustainable Income Streams On The Internet

With all that you'll learn and discover and carry out in the course, you should be excited about being one of the first to register as 'early bird' attendees.

In the **'Internet Infopreneur System'** coaching program, you're getting a set of skills you can use anytime, anywhere. No stone is left unturned. You'll get all the information you need to contain your losses, maximize your profits and access fully documented details on how to build an information product business on the Internet.

The simple, turnkey marketing system you build will keep your infopreneur business running 24 hours a day, whether you're in the office, away on holiday, or even at home asleep!

Is This Right For You?

Learn more about the program and decide for yourself. You'll find all the information you need about "The Internet Infopreneur System" at

http://www.InternetInfopreneur.com

So, Are You Ready To Succeed As An Infopreneur?

I hope you answered "YES".

Prepare and Plan To Succeed

A few months ago, my young daughter wanted a Barbie doll. I refused to buy her one. After a lot of 'power negotiating', we arrived at a deal. If she raised one half of the money she needed to buy her doll, I'd pitch in with the rest.

What happened next amazed me.

She drafted out a plan to create hand-made cards, and sold them to relatives and friends. She first calculated how many cards she needed to sell, then figured out long it would take to create them; and then went out and did it.

Within a month, she had raised the money – a considerable sum. Now she has her Barbie doll.

The secret is simple: Prepare and Plan.

To succeed in your infopreneur business, you too need a plan.

Decide how much you want to earn from your effort, and in what time. Estimate what kind of money you can reasonably make from the income streams you intend to include in your content. Calculate how many pages of content you'll need, how much traffic these pages will have to receive, and what kind of time investment is required to create them and drive traffic to them.

Analyze your own resources and skills. Do you have what it takes to create content websites or other forms of information products ? If not, can you find them or buy them or have someone create them for you? What new things will you need to learn?

Be realistic. Factor in delays in receiving payment from Adsense or affiliate merchants, the time it takes to get your site indexed in search engines, and the upfront costs you will incur in web hosting, marketing, tools and software. Don't expect cash to start pouring in tomorrow, or even next week. It may not happen.

Modify your plan often. As you grow and gain experience, you'll see that some ideas are good, and many are bad. Be ready and willing to modify your plan. Stay focused on your goal, and you'll stand a better chance of succeeding.

Why have I chosen to focus on these points in this book? The reason is simple. In my experience, these are far more important than the nuts and bolts of building websites and promoting them. That part is technical. Learn it once, follow the steps, and you'll get the job done.

But if it is really such a simple process, why is it that not many folks succeed big-time with it?

I wrote and distributed a short report called Content Profit Secrets. More than 2,000 people downloaded and read it. Over 100 testimonials poured in. I'm willing to bet that no more than 50 readers will actually take action on even one-half of what I teach in it. And the sad truth is, only five of them will actually stick with it for long enough to make the system massively profitable for them.

The single multifaceted reason for this difference is:

* mindset and preparation
* passion and purpose
* planning and action.

Be different. Decide to succeed. You will change your life.

I wish you every success, dear Infopreneur!

All success,

Dr. Mani
The Internet Infopreneur
http://InternetInfopreneur.com

Quick Order Form

You can quickly and conveniently order a copy of this book (in print or digital form) by using one of these options:

Email orders: orders@ThinkWriteRetire.com

Please mention the number of copies you want to order, and whether you want print books or digital ebooks. We will reply with details about completing your order within 3 business days.

Web orders:

From our website:
http://ThinkWriteRetire.com/book.htm

From Amazon.com:
http://Amazon.com

You can place your order using this website any time of the day or night. Your order will be processed instantly. For details on delivery time for print books, please view the site for details.

Bulk orders:

If you wish to place orders for multiple copies, please contact us via email for details about pricing, discounts and shipping.

Request Free Information

Please send FREE information about:

☐ Other books   ☐ Home study programs

☐ Mailing lists   ☐ Consulting

Name:

Address:

City:

State:

ZIP:

Country:

Email address:

Email your form to orders@ThinkWriteRetire.com

About The Author

Dr.Mani Sivasubramanian is a pediatric heart surgeon who uses his infopreneur business to fund heart surgery for under-privileged children.

He lives in India and treats little children born with congenital heart defects. Heart surgery is expensive. Many of his patients, from poor families, cannot afford the cost of treatment. So Dr.Mani decided to try and help sponsor the operations.

This was the simple concept behind an online adventure that started in 1996.

Ten years later, Dr.Mani's team had raised over $130,000 and funded heart surgery in 47 children, with many more to follow. He's well on his way to achieve an ambitious mission - to make high quality heart health care accessible and affordable to every Indian child.

Dr.Mani is also an experienced infopreneur and online marketing expert, owner of the popular Ezine Marketing Center and author of many ebooks, reports, tutorials, home study courses and print publications spanning various facets of building and growing a small business using the power of the Internet.

He has influenced countless e-publishers, home business owners and Internet marketers with his powerful writing, insight and experience, and is an enthusiastic crusader of what's possible for small home business owners by effectively harnessing the force of the World Wide Web.

Among other things, Dr.Mani has been named as one of Seth Godin's '99 Purple Cows' for innovative and remarkable marketing, and FAST COMPANY magazine has profiled his philanthropy-fuelled approach to business. He has consistently ranked in the list of top 50 Internet marketing specialists at Gurudaq. com

Dr.Mani was prompted to write this book because so many other infopreneurs and online marketers wanted to know his secret to turning words into wealth.

Now he is sharing it with you - the good life of being an infopreneur!

3064688

Made in the USA